Brilliant Ideas for Using ICT in the Inclusive Classroom

Shortlisted as a Finalist in the 2013 Educational Resources Awards, *Brilliant Ideas for Using ICT in the Inclusive Classroom* provides lots of simple, practical ideas showing teachers and support staff how they can use ICT to boost the achievement of all pupils.

This practical teachers' guide will help you to unlock the enormous potential of new technology in order to enhance pupils' learning, particularly for young people with additional needs. Written by two of the UK's leading technology experts, this invaluable and newly updated resource will enable you to use ICT effectively to make lessons more accessible, motivating and fun.

With 50 illustrated case studies and 20 starter activities, this practical resource will help you to introduce new technology into the inclusive classroom. It has been specifically designed to help develop your pupils' key skills, such as problem solving, developing concepts and communicating to different audiences. In each activity, the authors show why and how a particular resource was used and show how similar techniques can be implemented to open up the curriculum to your learners.

The authors include timely and realistic advice on how to use a range of technologies from the cheap and cheerful – and even free – to more sophisticated and specialist packages. Find out about:

- apps
- blogging
- digital animation
- podcasting
- digital storytelling
- wikis
- geocaching
- coding
- games and gaming
- satellite navigation
- art packages
- Twitter.

Whether you're already techno-savvy or looking to get started with ICT, this book is full of brilliant ideas on how to engage learners of all abilities using technology. If you're looking for inspiration on how to integrate creative uses of ICT with the curriculum, this book will prove invaluable.

Sally McKeown is an award-winning journalist and author who specialises in disability. She has taught in schools and colleges, supporting students with a wide range of learning needs, and now runs training courses for charities and educators.

Angela McGlashon is a former teacher, Senior Lecturer at Anglia Ruskin University and the University of Essex, local authority adviser, business manager and trainer for a variety of software companies. She is now a freelance consultant working with many mainstream and special schools.

nasen is a professional membership association that supports all those who work with or care for children and young people with special and additional educational needs. Members include teachers, teaching assistants, support workers, other educationalists, students and parents.

nasen supports its members through policy documents, journals, its magazine *Special!*, publications, professional development courses, regional networks and newsletters. Its website contains more current information such as responses to government consultations. **nasen**'s published documents are held in very high regard both in the UK and internationally.

Other titles published in association with the National Association for Special Educational Needs (nasen):

Language for Learning in the Secondary School: A Practical Guide for Supporting Students with Speech, Language and Communication Needs
Sue Hayden and Emma Jordan
2012/pb: 978-0-415-61975-2

Assessing Children with Specific Learning Difficulties: A Teacher's Practical Guide
Gavin Reid, Gad Elbeheri and John Everatt
2012/pb: 978-0-415-67027-2

Using Playful Practice to Communicate with Special Children
Margaret Corke
2012/pb: 978-0-415-68767-6

The Equality Act for Educational Professionals: A Simple Guide to Disability and Inclusion in Schools
Geraldine Hills
2012/pb: 978-0-415-68768-3

More Trouble with Maths: A Teacher's Complete Guide to Identifying and Diagnosing Mathematical Difficulties
Steve Chinn
2012/pb: 978-0-415-67013-5

Dyslexia and Inclusion: Classroom Approaches for Assessment, Teaching and Learning, Second Edition
Gavin Reid
2012/pb: 978-0-415-60758-2

Provision Mapping: Improving Outcomes in Primary Schools
Anne Massey
2012/pb: 978-0-415-53030-9

Beating Bureaucracy in Special Educational Needs: Helping SENCOs Maintain a Work/Life Balance, Second Edition
Jean Gross
2012/pb: 978-0-415-53374-4

Promoting and Delivering School-to-School Support for Special Educational Needs: A Practical Guide for SENCOs
Rita Cheminais
2013/pb: 978-0-415-63370-3

Time to Talk: Implementing Outstanding Practice in Speech, Language and Communication
Jean Gross
2013/pb: 978-0-415-63334-5

Brilliant Ideas for Using ICT in the Inclusive Classroom

Second edition

Sally McKeown and Angela McGlashon

LONDON AND NEW YORK

Helping Everyone Achieve ■■■

Second edition published 2015
by Routledge
2 Park Square, Milton Park, Abingdon, Oxon OX14 4RN

and by Routledge
711 Third Avenue, New York, NY 10017

Routledge is an imprint of the Taylor & Francis Group, an informa business

First edition published by David Fulton Publishers 2012

British Library Cataloguing in Publication Data
A catalogue record for this book is available from the British Library

Library of Congress Cataloging in Publication Data
McKeown, Sally.
Brilliant ideas for using ICT in the inclusive classroom / Sally McKeown and Angela McGlashon. – 2nd Edition.
pages cm
1. Educational technology. 2. Information technology–Study and teaching. 3. Inclusive education. I. McGlashon, Angela. II. Title.
LB1028.3.M398 2015
371.33–dc23
2014020622

ISBN: 978-1-138-82142-2 (hbk)
ISBN: 978-1-138-80902-4 (pbk)
ISBN: 978-1-315-75025-5 (ebk)

Typeset in Times New Roman
by Saxon Graphics Ltd, Derby

Printed and bound by CPI Group (UK) Ltd, Croydon, CR0 4YY

Contents

v

Foreword

Caroline Wright

When you talk to schools and senior managers from other countries you begin to realise that in the UK we have developed an approach to ICT in education that is the envy of the world. There are many reasons for this. Developers are very close to their market in the UK so they can respond to teachers' needs, make resources which are relevant to changes in policy and produce them in a timely fashion.

Since the first edition of *Brilliant Ideas for Using ICT in the Inclusive Classroom* the education sector has been through a number of challenges but has also experienced an incredibly positive phase of collaboration. Soon after the arrival of the coalition government in 2010 the education sector in England was put on hold while we waited for the details of the new curriculum. For two years teachers felt unable to prepare new teaching plans and suppliers and publishers could not invest in new product development without knowing what would be on the curriculum in future years. There was a feeling that we were all treading water without making any progress. Finally, in the summer of 2013, details of the new curriculum arrived and with incredible speed, and a little help from BESA, suppliers were able to develop new curriculum aligned resources and teachers started the first phase of classroom implementation. This has been no easy feat.

Not only did the changes demand a wide scale revision of teachers' lesson plans, but they also called for a new set of skills from teachers. One example was the new computer science curriculum. Pupils at KS1 are now required to create and debug simple programs and to understand algorithms and how they are implemented as programs on digital devices. Teachers were understandably nervous about taking on a subject such as this when they did not necessarily have the knowledge themselves. Companies such as Espresso and Rising Stars set to and developed resources that schools could use to meet the new requirements and, more importantly, which they could adapt in a creative way to combine computer science with topics in history or English.

But first rate content is only part of the solution. Teachers need tools. With an emphasis on raising standards and personalising learning, teachers need to have an increasingly sophisticated selection of options at their disposal. Now more than ever they need to be able to turn their skills to creating just the right resource which will help an individual child make that breakthrough.

Here they need help. In the past they had to be familiar with word processing, software for interactive whiteboards, and perhaps Logo, a database and spreadsheets. Now we expect them to have a much wider knowledge of software and hardware – everything from apps for tablets to animation to Twitter – and to be able to use all these resources creatively to improve teaching in the classroom. That is where a book such as *Brilliant Ideas for Using ICT in the Inclusive Classroom* is invaluable. It shows what real teachers are achieving in real classrooms and will raise the bar of expectations. The 50 Brilliant Ideas cover early years to further education with lots of key ideas for introducing technology one step at a time while the 20 Brilliant Starters give teachers the skills and confidence to do it for themselves.

The significant changes in policy over the past few years have been hard to address, but have fuelled a positive partnership between teachers, schools and suppliers. Coupled with this, we have the emergence of new and innovative ways of involving parents in learning. We may not want to see our parents turning into 'tiger mums' but the benefit of parental involvement to a child's development is a given.

Brilliant Ideas for Using ICT in the Inclusive Classroom is a wonderful showcase of what can be achieved when technology is used efficiently and effectively in schools. For this to happen we need to make sure that suppliers continue to talk to teachers to make sure that they really understand their needs. Never have we seen such a level of collaboration and, in turn, an increasing quality in learning resources. We are certainly at an exciting stage of education evolution.

Caroline Wright is director of BESA (British Educational Suppliers Association).

Acknowledgements

MANY PEOPLE CONTRIBUTED to this book. Particular thanks are due to Dr Linda Evans, Editor of *SENCO Update*, who suggested the original idea and Daniel McKeown for first line editing and research.

Thanks also to: Rob Havercroft – St Gabriel's School Newbury; Jack Todhunter – Newman School Rotherham; Mark Slawinski – Culture24; Michael Leeming – Storrington & District Museum Society; Lindsay Nadin – Pearson; Julie Wilson – Sore Thumb Marketing; Springwood Heath Primary School Liverpool; staff at plasq.com; Peter Everett – Whitmore Junior School Basildon; staff and pupils at Grangehurst School Coventry; David Mitchell blogger; Janine Foster – Stephenson Memorial Primary School in Wallsend; Katelyn McKeown and members of RASAG (Sheffield Refugee Asylum Seeker Action Group); Brendan Routledge – Suffolk Education Consultants; Crays Hill School in Essex; Brian Greene Gigajam; Arc School Nuneaton; Cotswold Community School; Anna Hughes – The Nuneaton Academy; National Association for Teaching English (NATE); Nick Day Orwell High School in Felixstowe; Sean O'Sullivan – Frank Wise School in Banbury; Jennette Holden – Pendle View School Lancashire; Jamie Munro – Inclusive Technology; Rebecca Cole – Glenaire Primary School in Shipley; Reeza Awoodun – Teched Marketing; Julie Yaxley – independent dyslexia consultant; Carol Weale – Dane Court Grammar School Broadstairs; Dorin Park School Cheshire; Gillian Penny – Gavinburn Primary School West Dunbartonshire; James Betts – Kudlian software; Sheila Robson – Priestnall Ach Stockport; Alison Carter – Longwill School for the Deaf in Birmingham; Chris Dunn – Grange Primary in Gloucester; Huw Williams – Avantis; Marilyn Mitchell – Mayfield Special School in Torbay; Alice Wyatt – Schools Library Service Warwickshire; Andrea Carr – Rising Stars; Jenny Langley the Manchester Academy; Emma Chandler; Tracy Playle – Pickle Jar Comms; James Langley – Bradford Metropolitan Borough Council; Jen Deyenberg (blogger at @jdeyenberg; Rosie Murphy – Fairfield School in Batley; Gavin Calnan – Bentleywood School Harrow; Sandra Miller – FACCT in Fife; Pauline Winter – Clapham Terrace Primary Warwickshire; Helen Davis – Davison C of E High School for Girls in Worthing; K.C. Kelly-Markwick – Oakwood Court College in Devon; Matt Rogers – Snowsfields Primary School in Bermondsey; Sarah Swain – Mydas PR and Marketing Limited; Jane Mitchell – CALSC; Rachel Lewis – Darwen Aldridge Community Academy; Matt Hartley – pfeg; Declan Wilkes – MyBnk; Alan Brown – Kingsmead School Derby; Andrea Keightley – Montsaye Community College in Northamptonshire; Stuart Porter – TrueTube; Carol Allen – advisory teacher for ICT and special needs in North Tyneside; Dawn Hallybone and Alissa Chesters – Oakdale Junior School in the London Borough of Redbridge; Nathan Cresswell – Pioneer School Essex; Debbie La – Montrose Road Centre Forfar; Dr Benjaman Schogler – Skoogmusic Limited; Katy Wilkinson – Oak Field School and Sports College Nottingham; Cameron Wade – Wizelearning; James Betts – Kudlian software; Clare Dibble – Oakdale Junior School in Redbridge; Yvonne Aylott – Westfield Technology College in Weymouth; Becky Ludlow – Moulton Primary School in Northamptonshire; Matt Fenn; Sue Greenwood – Tupton Hall School, Chesterfield; Sue Stevens; Ross Wallis at Sidcot School, Somerset; staff at Mary Hare School for the Deaf Newbury; Joe Beech; Sue Greenwood – Tupton Hall School Chesterfield; Cuckmere House School Seaford, East Sussex; madeinme; Professor Diana Laurillard from the London Knowledge Lab; Simrat Navi St Giles' Church of England Primary School Willenhall; Danny Nicolson, ICT Consultant Southend; Lorraine Petersen OBE; staff at Livewire PR; staff at Mango Marketing.

Part 1
Brilliant Ideas

Brilliant Idea 1

A tale of Tigtag, iPads and invertebrates

HOW DO YOU get pupils to revise for science without relying on written notes? Rob Havercroft, subject leader for science for juniors and e-learning coordinator at St Gabriel's School in Newbury, found that a judicious use of iPads, apps and an online multimedia resource meant that pupils got better results than ever before.

Classification is very important and helps children to think like scientists. They begin to look beyond surface differences to understand the relationship between living things. It can be a dry topic but with a good blend of videos and practical activities it is possible to make classification a creative, as well as an analytical task.

In the past schools might have used a textbook or photocopied worksheets, supplemented with a selection of websites and film clips from the BBC. Rob decided to use Tigtag, a primary science resource from a company called Twig World. Tigtag has 600 short films called 'tidbits' which last about one minute and core films of about three minutes, long enough to sustain interest but not so long

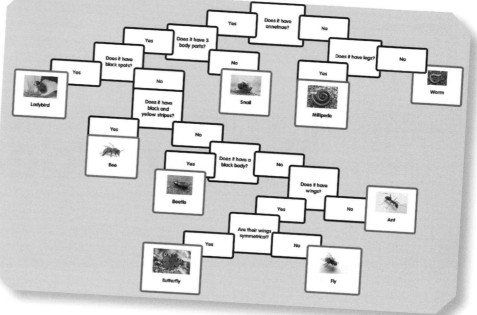

that they dominate the lesson. Tigtag seems to have all the elements a teacher might want to use: lesson plans, interactive whiteboard visuals and classroom activities, and everything is matched to the primary science curriculum. All the materials are produced to a high standard by researchers and subject experts, professional film makers and designers.

There are many good additional features. Key points appear on screen in a freeze frame at different stages and Rob has found that many girls like to take a photo on their iPads. This distils the crucial messages and the visuals give them a context and help them remember the content more dearly. Teachers can switch on captions. This not only helps pupils with a hearing loss but also those who are learning English and they do better if they can see and hear the language.

Armed with some knowledge of invertebrates, the girls went out into the school grounds and took pictures on their iPads. This meant that they left the animals in situ but their pictures gave a close up view of the creatures and let the viewer see something of their habitat too.

'One of the most powerful functions of the iPads is to be able to take pictures,' said Rob. 'One girl has filled her

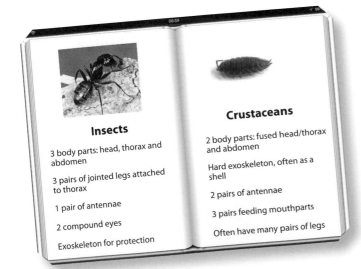

Insects

3 body parts: head, thorax and abdomen

3 pairs of jointed legs attached to thorax

1 pair of antennae

2 compound eyes

Exoskeleton for protection

Crustaceans

2 body parts: fused head/thorax and abdomen

Hard exoskeleton, often as a shell

2 pairs of antennae

3 pairs feeding mouthparts

Often have many pairs of legs

iPad already. She's done very well as it is the 32gb version and we only got them a couple of months ago.'

Once the girls had their photos, he asked them to choose six pictures of different creatures. They were introduced to the idea of a branching key to develop their own classification system using an app called Popplet on the iPads. They practised this as a group working with information about penguins but once they had got the idea they developed their own system of classification with questions such as: Does it have a shell? Does it have six legs?

Finally the girls made their own e-books with an app called Book Creator. Just as they might gather together all their handwritten notes in one folder, so with an e-book they can bring together all their electronic resources in one place. They collected photographs, stills from lessons, recordings of Rob's explanations, instructions, group discussions, video clips and links to websites. This means they have a very rich resource, which they remember because they have created it for themselves.

Not only are the final results impressive but they also have had a good effect on pupils' performance. Recently they had an examination. 'One of the girls was nervous and thought she could not answer the questions,' said Rob. 'Then she remembered that she had made a film about the lung. As she thought about her video, it all came back and she was able to get full marks.'

iPads add a new dimension as pupils can:

- ✔ Access information in multimedia form.
- ✔ Produce multimedia responses
- ✔ Take pictures of displays or whiteboards.
- ✔ Video classroom activities.
- ✔ Dictate their ideas.
- ✔ Produce a movie.
- ✔ Use an app for mind mapping.
- ✔ Make their notes on screen with embedded links.

A longer version of this article was originally published as 'Tag the invertebrates' in *Primary Teacher Update*, Vol. 01, Iss. 24, September 2013, pp. 52–53: www.primaryteacherupdate.co.uk. This extract is reproduced by kind permission of the publishers MA Education.

Contacts and information

Tigtag from Twig World: www.twig-world.co.uk/tigtag/
Popplet: http://popplet.com/
Book Creator: https://itunes.apple.com/

Brilliant Idea 2

Disney and Spielberg need to look to their laurels

NEWMAN SCHOOL IN Rotherham is a Specialist School for Cognition and Learning. A few years ago Jack Todhunter, former teacher of English at the school, started to use Apple technology with the program I Can Animate. Since then, the school has won a number of awards for its work with claymation and digital animation.

'*Theseus and the Minor Detour* was one of our first attempts,' said Jack, 'and although we have moved on, we are still very fond of it. We were amused when someone at Cambridge University cited it as a good example of getting children to engage with the classics! So far as they were concerned it was just a good story and fun to animate.'

'I always feel we should encourage "stealth reading" where pupils engage with a variety of texts but don't realise how hard they are working,' said Jack. 'At the moment we are animating the witches' scene in *Macbeth* and in the past we have worked on *King Lear*, *Othello*, *Wuthering Heights*, *Great Expectations* – not many mainstream schools could claim as much.'

Newman School had two entries in the National Schools Film and Animation Awards run by TAG Learning Limited. *Homage to Hitch* features a strange bird which 'haunts' a couple of villagers and was the culmination of work on Daphne Du Maurier and Alfred Hitchcock. The storyboard itself emanated from a genuine article in the *Daily Mail* which, by happy coincidence, was published in the middle of the project. As preparation for the piece, the students had to ground themselves in a number of genres including short story, film and journalism before turning their hand to animation. The result is a story full of suspense and humour. Their second competition entry was *Safety on the Internet*, which combines drawings, computer graphics, avatars and synthetic speech to create a short piece with a very futuristic feel.

The whole process is very engaging. Creating the models in clay is quite therapeutic for those children who can be hyperactive and they all really enjoy the 'making' part of the process. 'When we made *Homage to Hitch*, we had several versions of the clay figures which were farmed out around the class. We storyboarded the action and people could choose which parts they wanted to animate and edit. It was a very collaborative approach. After all, at Aardman Animations, the company that produced *Wallace and Gromit*, they have a team of 60 or so animators so we should aim to work in the same way. We also had a parents' evening and let them animate a couple of frames so they got a feeling for the skills involved. Some parents were so taken with the project that they have bought computers and animation software to use at home.'

You could:

- ✔ Host inter-school competitions.
- ✔ Use it for after-school clubs.
- ✔ Make it a feature of transition activities where primary and secondary pupils come together.
- ✔ Hold community events
- ✔ Animate a story, poem or song.
- ✔ Use finger puppets to use as animation characters.
- ✔ Animate inanimate objects such as pens, knives and forks or Lego.
- ✔ Animate a process in history or science, such as mummifying in Egypt or birds making a nest.
- ✔ Use a visualiser to animate ice melting, flowers fading or mould growing by utilising the delayed snapshot on the visualiser.
- ✔ Capture the movements of the class pet as it moves around the bowl or cage.

Contacts and information

Newman School has used a range of software for their work:
Crazy Talk 6 – www.taglearning.com
I Can Animate – www.kudlian.net/
Noodle Flix – http://noodle-flix.en.softonic.com/mac
Xtranormal – www.xtranormal.com/
Claymation – www.ikitmovie.com/59/claymation.htm

See the videos online at:
Theseus and the Minor Detour
www.youtube.com/watch?v=YMPDOcohcLY

Homage to Hitch
http://schoolstube.com/asset/view/id/937/code/1eec34

Brilliant Idea 3

Visit museums online and become a Caboodle curator!

SO MANY ARTEFACTS which represent the nation's heritage are to be found in museums. They give us a unique insight into our past, from the agricultural traditions in Britain to the conditions for slaves coming into Liverpool before heading out to the New World. These days it can be really hard to organise school trips on a regular basis. A project called Caboodle, run by Culture24, opens up some of the best museums to children and gives them the chance to develop some curator skills with collections of their own.

Mark Slawinski, Staff Writer and Outreach Co-ordinator at Culture24 explains what Caboodle can offer: 'Caboodle is Culture24's fun, free and safe collections website for children. On it, children become digital curators to exhibit their precious things as well as photos of the world around them. Caboodle is a website which lets young people become digital curators, collecting and exchanging collections of digital photos.'

'It is free but you need to sign up to it and then you can submit an endless stream of digital images. These collections could be stickers, Lego, clothing, shells, artwork, bike bits, books or anything which interests you. Caboodle guides offer the following categories: Arty, Nature, People, Random, Toys and Treasures, but users can add their own.'

Some museums are already heavily involved: the Royal Armouries have already Caboodled two sets of outstanding content including Elephant Armour, Henry VIII's 'Horned Helmet' and a mysterious and exotic 'Dasta Bungha' from the sixteenth century. There are many amazing museum objects on the site to inspire children. They may then create a set in response, learn new facts about the nation's treasures or be inspired to start a new collection of their own.

Other museums have signed up and opened their doors to the Caboodle project. One of the really exciting aspects of the site is its ability to allow young people to have fun describing collection items on a museum's behalf. Storrington Museum in West Sussex recently let a group of young Caboodlers take photos of their collection, and the resulting Caboodle can be seen in various categories on the site.

Caboodle presents a fun opportunity for museums to 'repackage' a sample from their collections. We've had three great sets from English Heritage, a sample of the Designated Collection from the Horniman Museum along with their must-see giant walrus, and various action-packed Caboodles from the Jorvik Viking Centre and The Shakespeare Birthplace Trust.

You could:

- ✔ Link to the local museum and ask them to visit.
- ✔ Find a Caboodle and create activities around it.
- ✔ As a class make a Caboodle and post it online.
- ✔ Run an after-school Curators' Club.
- ✔ Use it as an opportunity for children who are experts on a topic to showcase their knowledge.
- ✔ Using an art package, select, copy and paste part of an exhibit to create a pattern.
- ✔ Put a colour wash over an object.
- ✔ Use special effects to create an Impressionist or Pop Art version.
- ✔ Create a museum of your own with labels.
- ✔ Record labels for your museum.
- ✔ Make a photostory (using Photo Story 3 from Microsoft).
- ✔ Use the images to create sorting activities.
- ✔ Use the images to make a quiz.
- ✔ Make a treasure trail by putting images around for pupils to find.
- ✔ Give some clues for pupils to identify the correct image.
- ✔ Make a 'what could this be used for?' quiz.

Contacts and information
www.caboodle.org.uk
www.show.me.uk

Brilliant Idea 4

Taking a dip in the summer months

St Mary's Academy is a two-form entry primary school in Suffolk. Like most schools, it generally finds a 'dip' in reading progress between the end of one year and the next. In the summer of 2012, Kate Ruttle, the SENCO at St Mary's Academy carried out a project to see if access to Bug Club would impact on the 'summer holiday dip' between Year 2 and Year 3.

'In July 2012, we designated Class I our intervention class, giving them access to www.bugclub.co.uk. The other class in this year group were not given access to Bug Club during the summer to see if there was a measurable difference between the two classes.'

In order to find out whether Bug Club had an impact on the children's reading levels, they assessed all the children's reading abilities prior to and following the summer holidays by measuring with National Curriculum levels and a phonics test.

They found that in the class using Bug Club, no children 'dipped' and 56 per cent made reading progress. In contrast, in the class not using Bug Club during the summer months, 11 per cent 'dipped' and only 46 per cent made reading progress.

This followed a similar project carried out to find out how to support boys' reading. Boys' literacy has been a key area of concern for some time. There is a shortage of male role models in primary settings with a preponderance of female teachers, so reading is sometimes seen as something that girls do. But computer reading schemes can seem more real for some children and the virtual book bag is always to hand so the cry of 'I left my book at school' just doesn't cut it.

Bug Club from Pearson features well-known characters such as Wallace and Gromit. Children might read the books in print form or go for the online version which they can access on any computer with an internet connection. They can also earn Bug points for completing interactive reading activities and then exchange these points for rewards such as decorating their own tree-house or growing their own dragon. It seems that for some boys the element of competition is very motivating.

All of the children in school have daily phonics sessions in attainment sets. Charlie, a very active little boy, has always been unwilling to sit down, to read and to write. Assessments suggest that he has low average receptive vocabulary and a poor short-term memory. He was doing the phase 3 work for the third time because he hadn't made the progress we had hoped for. This had previously been put down to his behaviour but it quickly became apparent that part of Charlie's difficulty was that he didn't 'get' the point of phonics.

'By the end of Year 1, he was realising that he was falling behind his peers and his behaviour worsened,' said Kate Ruttle. 'This pattern continued at the beginning of Year 2 and we were hesitant about taking him into the programme. However, he was really keen because he liked the idea of reading the Star Wars books or the Wallace and Gromit books.'

For Charlie, the value of Bug Club is twofold: the small steps in the Bug Club let him make progress without fear of failure, and the clusters of books give him incentives to move on. Charlie's behaviour is now much improved and he is generally willing to make an attempt at anything that is offered to him – including writing, which was once a significant trigger for temper tantrums.

Although he is still working below the expected level for his age, Charlie is now learning to learn and enjoying becoming a reader.

Brilliant Idea 5

Chatting about Miss Havisham

IT IS SOMETIMES hard to motivate students, so tapping into interests such as online chat can be a really good way to engage them. Anna Hughes taught poetry to a mixed ability Year 8/9 transition group who were about to start their GCSE course at Caludon Castle School in Coventry. Here she reports on how using a wiki had unexpected results.

'The first step of the project was to create and develop the webspace. Although this sounds daunting, it really isn't difficult. I was pleasantly surprised at how quickly I got to grips with it.' (See the 'How to use a Wiki' help sheet if you are interested in setting up your own.)

'The transition scheme that I was using with my Year 8s had a section on poetry with a focus on the poem "Havisham" by Carol Ann Duffy. I uploaded the poem to the wiki and created a page with a number of resources that I would normally have delivered to the class myself: a PowerPoint about the poem which I had previously delivered to other classes, a set of questions, some notes in a Word document and two links to useful websites which analysed the poem. I showed the students how to use the site, got them signed up with their own usernames and then they had to use the resources to answer some fairly difficult questions.

'I also briefly introduced the students to the discussion pages and encouraged them to communicate with each other. This worked amazingly well because it gave them an opportunity to share their views or ask questions that they wouldn't necessarily have wanted to do in the open classroom. It helped that they could hide behind their "online identity". I knew who they were as I had access to everyone's username, but other students didn't (unless they decided to share this with others) so they took a risk and had a go at parts of the poem that they found hard.

'Some pupils were contributing when normally they would have kept quiet. If I had taught them the poem, they would have followed my guidance and most likely would have ended up with my interpretation of the poem. Instead, they came up with really unusual, original responses. Most importantly, students were now interrogating the poem themselves, asking questions and explaining things to each other. A number of students posted questions asking for help reading the meaning of different lines from the poem; these were promptly answered and explained by others in the class. Suddenly, it seemed there was no need for me!'

This case study is based on a project undertaken for the National Association for Teaching English (NATE).

A fuller version can be accessed at: www.nate.org.uk/htt. We are grateful to NATE for their permission to include the project here.

You could:

- ✔ Make an online collaborative space to examine a problem such as bullying, making friends or other SEAL topics.
- ✔ Use a debating forum for a current topic in the news.
- ✔ Use it to provide the background for a topic being studied in school, i.e. ask students to find out as much as they can about China and then review the results the next day.

Contact and information

http://primarypad.com

Brilliant Idea 6

Using the technology to teach touch typing

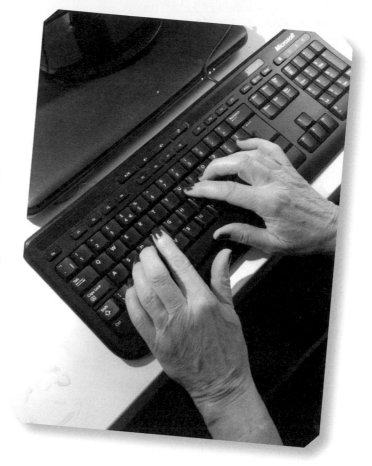

O NCE UPON A time, touch typing was taught in many schools. These days, despite the ubiquity of laptops, we often see children using the much less effective hunt-and-peck method of using a keyboard. This usually involves two-finger typing, is not rhythmic and does not encourage or develop a kinaesthetic approach.

Keyboarding is the foundation of so much work with technology and has other advantages too. Once children can touch type they unconsciously associate patterns on the keyboard with the spelling of certain words. As one girl said, '"was" is a triangle and "were" is three steps forward and one back.'

Touch-type Read and Spell (TTRS) and Kaz are among the best known packages. TTRS proved very effective with a group of pupils with visual impairments. Chris had monocular vision, reduced visual acuity in his dominant eye, poor literacy skills, difficulties staying on task, poor concentration and poor listening skills. He was always the first to arrive and generally stayed on task and managed to get a 100 per cent score after he had attended 19 classes. He was delighted. So were his tutor and parents because Chris does not cope well with delayed gratification.

He began to touch type both at home and in school. There were other benefits: his literacy skills developed and he became so much more confident that he felt able to offer support to other children in his class with spelling difficulties. His listening and concentration skills became more consistent too.

Kaz is endorsed by the British Dyslexia Association and uses proper words from the very beginning, not mindless strings of letters. It is quick and easy to follow with a little bird on screen to guide learners through the exercises. Children can get going without having to read through lots of written instructions.

Moat School is a small co-educational day school for children between the ages of 11 and 16 that specialises in support for dyslexic learners. Some of the children have low self-esteem when they first arrive at the school because they have not thrived in their previous schools. One thing that is different about Moat School is that children each have their own laptop and take it from lesson to lesson so good keyboarding skills are crucial.

'We use Kaz at the beginning of Year 7,' said Moat teacher Melanie Kling, 'to get the students going or to increase their speeds. They will use their laptop in every lesson and for homework too. Speed and accuracy are very important if they are to use their laptops successfully in examinations. Some of the children manage 70 wpm.'

Some children join the school later on and then they are given their own individual account to build their skills as fast as possible. Kaz has a very good logging system so staff can keep an eye on progress. Touch typing requires continual practice. Children can log on at home so learners can practise and keep their speeds up during the holidays.

Advantages of touch typing:

- ✔ Children can soon type faster than they can write.
- ✔ It develops a kinaesthetic approach to spelling so children remember patterns on the keyboard.
- ✔ It uses muscle memory so there is less physical fatigue.
- ✔ Looking at the screen and not the keys means the quality of writing is usually better.
- ✔ Children develop a sense of what feels right.
- ✔ It offers a chance to revisit phonics and the spelling of basic words in a new context so it is good revision.
- ✔ It separates transcription from composition so children just focus on one skill.

Contacts and information

TTRS: https://readandspell.com/

Kaz Typing tutor: www.kaz-type.com

Brilliant Idea 7

Androids and CapturaTalk narrow the achievement gap

CAPTURA**T**ALK FOR **A**NDROID will take a picture, then use optical character recognition (OCR) to turn print into text and read it aloud. This means that a pupil can take a picture of a textbook, a poster, a leaflet or website content and have it read out. It is especially useful for people on the move. Users can go to a museum, an airport or a public library with a tablet or a smartphone and have a discreet tool which lets them find out what written text says. They can also use it to read back their own compositions so they can get a clear picture of what they are writing. This is especially important for those learners who get stuck at word and sentence level composition and need extra support to create longer texts.

Liverpool's Springwood Heath Primary School, has more than 50 per cent of pupils with special needs. Some have speech and language delay, others social and emotional issues or specific learning difficulties.

CapturaTalk has been used extensively in literacy lessons because it helps children by reading back words and sentences and the highlighting facility is good for children with poor visual tracking. The children also like to use CapturaTalk's talking browser for research on the internet.

A teacher describes the impact on writing skills: 'I work with children in class who have difficulties understanding what they write. They have what they want to write in their head but what appears on paper is very different. We have children who will write a really interesting story, will tell you what it is but it doesn't bear any resemblance to what they have written and they can't read it back to you. With CapturaTalk they can hear the text as they are writing and correct it while they still have the ideas in their mind. They learn to identify where

the errors are and correct them. After just a few weeks of using the tablet we are seeing the children develop these strategies. We can see that this will help them work more independently in the future. I am now starting to use the speech feedback to check words that children don't understand when reading and I want to start to use the word prediction to extend their vocabulary and spelling skills.'

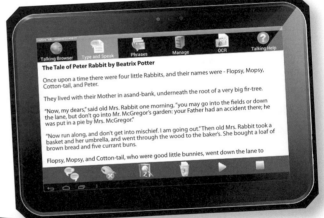

Advantages of CapturaTalk:

- ✔ Take a picture and convert printed words to digital text with OCR
- ✔ It is a highly motivating app.
- ✔ It reads the text back to them.
- ✔ They also find it easier as they are able to change the fonts and colours of the text.
- ✔ Type and listen back with text-to-speech.
- ✔ CapturaTalk will read aloud web, PDF and e-books with text-to-speech.
- ✔ Users can dictate and convert their words with Voice Recognition.
- ✔ It will transcribe audio files into typed text.
- ✔ It has an integral dictionary.
- ✔ Currently there are English, Spanish and German versions of CapturaTalk. You can also use the Translate feature to translate text to and from a wide range of languages.
- ✔ It can accelerate progress for GCSE learners.

Contact and information
CapturaTalk: www.capturatalk.com/103/about-capturatalk

Brilliant Idea 8

Put comics in the mix: improving narrative skills

COMIC BOOKS HAVE been blamed for declining standards in reading and writing and are sometimes viewed as not being 'proper books', but one school in Coventry has used them as part of their focus on improving the quality of writing, particularly among boys, ultimately lifting a critical number of pupils from level 3 into level 4.

Grangehurst is a large primary school in the north east of Coventry. The proportion of pupils eligible for free school meals is above average, as is the number identified as having learning difficulties or disabilities. About a fifth of pupils come from minority ethnic backgrounds although only a small number are in the early stages of learning English.

The school was keen to raise boys' attainment and to adopt more varied and interactive teaching styles. The project was based in two parallel Year 5 classes who were working on Narrative Unit 2: Traditional Stories, Fables, Myths and Legends. The teachers identified a group of underachieving children to target and track through the project. The majority of children in this group were boys.

The unit allowed for lots of cross-curricular ideas involving design and technology, history and science linked to the Robin Hood theme. At the writing phase children were offered a choice of ways to produce their own stories – The Adventures of Robin Hood – and all stories were to be published in a class book.

The use of ICT to produce a comic strip of their stories was highly motivating and the children were immensely proud of their work. This work also helped them to develop a good sense of a plot. One teacher reported: 'The children loved doing the comics. The fact that the pictures were of themselves made them even more interested and they were so proud of their work when they saw them printed. The comics helped children to get familiar with the story they were going to write and to separate narrative from speech. They were able to think about what was important to put into the speech bubbles, which then helped them later in their writing to think about the dialogue they would use.'

Whitmore Junior School in Basildon has used Comic Life for Social and Emotional aspects of Learning (SEAL). Pupils took the theme of rumours and produced a podcast and comic book to show how rumours and gossip could hurt people's feelings. They gathered together visuals and produced a script. One of the pupils said, 'All you do is drag pictures into a box, click onto a button and speech bubbles come up. Then you type in text and it turns into comic book.'

Teacher Peter Everett said, 'This gives them the opportunity to try something completely different and they don't realise how much their learning has developed as a result.'

You could:

✔ Use comic strips to relate any kind of narrative: eyewitness accounts for humanities or retelling a fairy tale, for example.

✔ Use for sequencing work for science or cookery with key ideas in speech bubbles.

✔ Create stories about Greek myths and legends (www.e2bn.org have a wonderful story creator).

✔ Create warning posters with captions.

✔ Create your own comic strip guide book to your school.

✔ Create labels for use around the school to turn off lights or taps.

✔ Create your own comic strip for a film or song you like.

Contacts and information

Comic Life: http://plasq.com
Garfield Comic Creator: www.garfield.com/fungames/comiccreator.html
http://garfield.com/game/comic-creator
Strip Generator: www.stripgenerator.com
http://stripgenerator.com/strip/create
Comic Brush: www.comicbrush.com
Comic Life and SEAL: www.heppell.net/bva/bva4/whitmorejunior.htm
How to use Comic Life in the Classroom – www.macinstruct.com/node/69
Children at Hackleton School using Comic Life at Silverstone – www.youtube.com/watch?v=JEQVYr-7MbU

Brilliant Idea 9

Blogging widens horizons

***D**AVID **M**ITCHELL OR @DeputyMitchell, as most people know him, is a prolific blogger, an ex head teacher and now advises schools on how to set up their own blogs. As he reports here, he became a blog convert when he saw a real jump in attainment and progress with a Year 6 group in Bolton.*

When I arrived at Heathfield School many children were disengaged and predicted levels were very low. Perhaps even more important was the parochialism of the pupils. Although the school is on the outskirts of Bolton, 30 per cent had not visited the centre and 80 per cent had never visited nearby Manchester. I was desperate to find something to motivate myself because I believe that if I am excited, they will be.

I started with certain key beliefs:

- Build it and they will come.
- Pupils will be patient.
- Parents will flock to see it.

None of these things happened. We could see who was reading the blog and week after week it was just people in Bolton. Then one day, we were working on numeracy when I heard a great intake of breath: 'New York! They are looking at our blog!' Sadly it turned out that there is a New York near Sunderland but we didn't tell the parents that. Now, after five years, our blog has reached an audience of 14,000.

What difference did it make to Year 6?

We were working on non-chronological report writing. We had looked at some examples and picked out the features of a good report. One boy was working at level 3b. He decided he was going to write about Howler monkeys and set out to find 13 facts. No one in the school knew anything although he did interrogate everyone he met in the corridor.

He put a request on the class blog and got an email from a man who said, 'My daughter is working in an animal sanctuary in Guatemala.' He used the school email account and contacted Sarah McSharry who sent him information and photos of a monkey called Harry. Within a few days his writing had improved so much that he was writing at level 4a. Over the rest of that year he wrote 150,000 words and filled 60 exercise books.

Another boy was very impulsive and outspoken and took little trouble over the niceties of writing so his work had no capital letters or full stops. He wrote a blog post about his art work and got a reply from someone in Australia saying, 'Great artwork but capitals and full stops would make it easier to understand.' I had made it clear on the blog that they had to do their best work: 'Anybody in the world can view our blog so it is important that you always try your best and not only spell words correctly but also remember your punctuation and choose your words carefully.' I was a little put out when he told me that my criticisms were not important: 'You're just a teacher. You're not real. Mr Gilbert has given up his spare time to leave me this comment.' It just goes to show that feedback is only authentic when it comes from the outside world.

What we learnt:

- ✔ You need to write a lot to improve writing.
- ✔ Blogging encourages children to write more.
- ✔ Even five-year-olds can write what they think about their lessons.
- ✔ Exchange blogs with places like Canada and Australia to make pupils aware of the wider world.
- ✔ When we encouraged pupils to write their own short stories some produced essays of 5,000 words or more.
- ✔ They find it fun and will go home and write long blog posts.

party European Social Fund event FLIP Food football Free funding FURD hate crime HLC Home Office Humber Learning Consortium Immigration Minister IT legends Lemlem Lemlem's Coming Home Lemlem Hussein Abdu libraries Mim Suleiman Northern Refugee Centre Old Junior School Pallav Roy performance picnic RASAG rasag launch refugees refugee week Section 4 Sharrow community forum Sheffield Sheffield City College Sheffield City Council Sheffield Community Network Side by Side Slavery Stop Destitution Starving Sheffield storytelling summer of sanctuary UKBA VIDEO

Lemlem was born in a village in 1950 in what is now Eritrea. She was married at 12 and spoke Tigrinyan. She lived a traditional life and was not able to read or write her native language. Lemlem was surrounded by her family and friends, parents, children, grandchildren… In 1978 her village was burned down. Lemlem lost everything. She fled. She survived.

This boy was part of a group we took to the BETT exhibition in London. At the end of our presentation to a packed audience he stepped forwards and said: 'Blogging has changed my life. It has taken me from the detention room every lunchtime to standing in front of you guys at the biggest ICT show in the world.'

The 100 word challenge

At Stephenson Memorial Primary School in Wallsend on Tyneside they have been using the 100 word challenge as a way into blogging.

Many children believe they have to write a lot to win approval and reluctant writers are deterred by the blank page. Twitter and the 100 word challenge offer many advantages for these pupils. When every word counts, children have to concentrate and pare down their writing. Once they have cut the waffle, they realise that the message becomes more succinct and effective. Children can experiment more with their writing without running out of stamina. In fact, the whole composition process becomes more manageable.

Not just for children

Social media activity has benefits for asylum seekers and refugees in Sheffield. It raises awareness of their circumstances, creates a public profile which showcases activities and contributions and lets them keep up to date with family, friends and events in their countries of origin. Many were reluctant to engage with social media at first because of lack of IT skills, poor internet access, fear of monitoring and surveillance and language barriers. By contributing to a shared blog space they can record evidence of activities, for example a short employment course, a weekly IT skills drop-in, or a project involving multiple volunteers.

Contacts and information

@DeputyMitchell http://y52012.heathfieldcps.net/tag/ y5-at-heathfield-primary-school-bolton/ http://deputymitchell.com/quadblogging/ 100 word challenge – 100wc.net RASAG: http://sheffieldrasag.wordpress.com

Brilliant Idea 10

Digital video for life stories

IT SEEMS TO be that digital storytelling as a medium is well suited to fostering a sense of kinship and community. It has an immediate appeal because it combines images, sound and text and gives us the sense of drawing back the curtain on someone else's life, if only for a few moments.

Brendan Routledge, a consultant with Suffolk Education Consultants, has worked with schools across the East of England and believes digital storytelling can change lives. Here he describes two instances where the end result more than justified the time and effort teachers and pupils put into learning how the technology worked.

Sinead was in Year 6 at Bishop Parker Primary School in Milton Keynes. She was unhappy, had a very poor self-image and was sidelined by many of her classmates. She never completed any work and was struggling both academically and socially. The school took part in a pilot project on digital storytelling run by the East of England Broadband Network. The brief was to tell a story, which had to be true, and to produce pictures or ideas for video clips which could be shot very quickly.

For some reason, this really captured Sinead's imagination and she told the story of her dog Rex from his days as a puppy, chewing her teddies and Barbies, through to his death. A lovable rogue, he brought down the curtains and opened the bathroom window until he got too old. When her story was shown to the rest of the class they saw her in a different light. She had become an individual and not just the surly girl at the back of the class who did as little as possible. Some of the boys started asking her to help them construct their Storyboards and to decide what

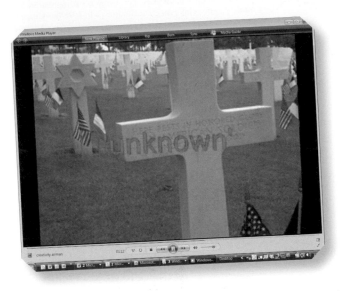

to include and how to tell their stories. Her confidence grew and this changed her attitude to reading and writing. She started to do things of her own accord instead of hanging back and feeling a failure.

Digital storytelling can also bridge the gap between generations. During the Second World War, there was an American airbase at Mendlesham. Stoke Ash Primary School in Suffolk used this for a KS2 project. They looked at local history books, correspondence and archive records. The pupils also visited the American War Cemetery at Madingley, near Cambridge, where they found the graves of airmen who had been based at their airfield. Last year they met a number of the veterans on their annual visit to the airfields of East Anglia.

The pupils produced digital stories based on individual airmen, particular planes and a tour of the airfield then and now. They also linked poems written by one of the airmen with digital images. The stories were eventually turned into a DVD with additional material, including video clips from a memorial service held at the school which was attended by senior US Air Force officers.

'The head teacher was able to travel to the USA in September and present the finished work to the veterans at their annual reunion,' said Brendan. 'This was a very emotional experience. The veterans were overwhelmed by the interest taken in their stories and by the quality of the work produced by such young children. Certainly this technology offers a rich resource and way of working for pupils who are not succeeding with more conventional methods.'

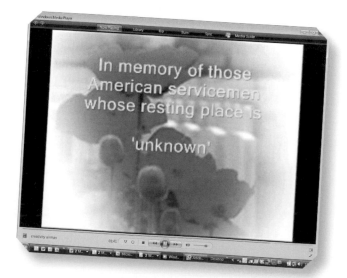

What makes a good digital story?

1. It should be short – people get restless after a few minutes and the story loses its power.
2. The best examples are based on personal experiences so that we learn something about the individual storytellers, their life and their attitudes.
3. Go for a few carefully chosen images, a voice-over and/ or background music and simple titling. Don't let the technology overwhelm the story.
4. Find sources of copyright-free music. In Suffolk the Regional Broadband Consortia (RBC) has entered into an agreement with the music production company Audio Network plc.
5. Get good pictures: these might be digital camera, scanned or drawn but the more pictures you have to choose from the better the end result.
6. Don't let the work drag on. Many pupils can make something quite good in a short space of time. Too much time leads to loss of impetus.

You could:

✔ Make videos about your daily routine, family, school or people who help us.
✔ Use a green screen behind your video to enable pupils to present information or stories while putting a photo behind them. Kudlian's I Can Present makes this very easy.
✔ Make a story starter video and ask 'what happens next?'
✔ Make video clips of a story and then ask students to put them in order.
✔ Ask pupils to make the letters in their names with their bodies and use as a quiz for the rest of the class.
✔ Take videos through different shape 'masks'... a keyhole, a door, a spyglass.

Contacts and information

Windows Movie Maker is free on most Windows machines.
However, schools may prefer to use iMovie (Mac), Pinnacle Studio or Premiere Elements.
They are all based on the same storyboard or timeline technology which is essential for planning and use the same special effects and transitions so pupils find it easy to transfer their skills.
Suffolk Education Consultants: www.suffolkeducationconsultants.net

Brilliant Idea 11

Tell me all about it: recording pupils' voices in place of writing!

Supplies for Schools

SOME CHILDREN FIND the task of recording their work through writing just too difficult. Teachers need to show what the child knows but up until now, writing it down has been the only option. But how about recording their observations or knowledge using a basic microphone/recorder such as the Easi-Speak?

Recording children's voices used to be hard work. Often a learning support assistant would sit in the corner of the room and press buttons while holding a microphone and urging a child to speak. The quality was not always good and it was very much a discrete activity cut off from the main classroom. Now it is so easy to integrate sound into a lesson in a much more natural way and 'roving' microphones let you record on the move and then plug into the computer once you are back in the classroom.

Crays Hill School in Essex has a high traveller intake. The KS1 teacher took the pupils out on a bug hunt using Easi-Speak microphones. At the end of the day the children sat enthralled as they listened to their classmates' descriptions and tried to identify their bug on a chart in the classroom.

'All at once,' their teacher said, 'children who would switch off in normal lessons were listening attentively, absorbing and retaining information and priding themselves on being first to identify the bug! So much follow-up work ensued, from charts and graphs to recorded stories about bugs. It was so much fun to see all the class included in the activities!'

Advantages

These digital voice recorders are very robust so you can use them with children of all ages as they will stand a few knocks. There is a built-in microphone and speaker and you can record, play back and skip files. Recordings can be made directly to MP3 which makes podcasting very easy or to WAV format and can be downloaded to a computer via USB.

You could:

- ✔ Use it to record, upload and re-record projects to assess progress.
- ✔ Use it for recording interviews, plays and information such as cooking activities.
- ✔ Record in your times table songs and rhymes for all the class to sing to.
- ✔ Use it to present mock radio programmes or school news items.
- ✔ Interview local residents or visitors to the school.
- ✔ Use it on field trips to record observations and reactions to different environments.
- ✔ Record and listen to music and sounds.
- ✔ Get the children's first reactions about sports days, singing or being in a school production.

Contact and information
www.tts-group.co.uk/

Brilliant Idea 12

'Living on a Prayer' with Gigajam

GIGAJAM IS A virtual learning environment with a difference. It teaches keyboard, guitar, bass and drums. Students have an individual log-in and can access the site at home and at school. They need to have an instrument to hand as they work through the tutorials, recording and improving their own efforts. There are 10 lessons for each instrument but these are broken down into many different modules and students can work at their own pace.

Arc School near Nuneaton is an independent specialist school for 35 boys and girls aged 11 to 14 who have behavioural problems which make it difficult for some of them to form good social relationships. Some have associated learning difficulties. Patrick Jackson teaches music both in class and on an individual basis.

Some students are keen to try all four instruments while others commit to one very early on. Patrick uses Gigajam a lot for the one-to-one sessions and finds that working with technology as well as having a tutor on hand helps a student make rapid progress.

Originally students wanted to be singers but since Gigajam was introduced, there are more instrumentalists emerging. Many students log on at home and, so long as parents are willing to take responsibility, students can borrow instruments to take home so they can continue practising.

Reece arrived at Arc School at the end of Year 6 and in just a few months he had worked through five lessons of Gigajam and all the associated modules. He has become an avid keyboard player and has been part of a

You could:

✔ Use Gigajam to supplement peripatetic music teaching.

✔ Use it to help students make quick progress in the early stages of learning an instrument.

✔ Use it for individual learning.

✔ Use Gigajam to help students develop the skills and confidence to form a band.

✔ Run a family learning workshop where parents and students learn and perform together.

✔ In Wandsworth a school took 20 Year 7 pupils of mixed ability, but no specific music skills and gave them four days of music tuition on a first and second instrument so that they could form a school rock band.

✔ Run after school clubs using Gigajam.

✔ Use it for transition projects so secondary pupils help children from primary schools learn the basics of a new instrument.

✔ One school used it as part of the Gifted and Talented programme.

newly formed band in the school. The high point this year was when Reece and the other band members went to a professional recording studio near Coventry to record the Bon Jovi classic 'Living on a Prayer'.

'They recorded their own parts and learnt how a track is laid down,' said Patrick, 'When I heard the final production, it was brilliant. It just blew me away. We will definitely be using Gigajam again next year.'

Advantages:

- It has a therapeutic effect on many learners.
- Students can upload their performances to an e-portfolio and share them with teachers, family and friends.
- Students can work at their own pace.
- It can be accessed at home and at school.
- It provides regular assessments.
- Students have clear evidence of progression.
- It can be used as a tool to build and strengthen professional relationships.

Contacts and information

http://gigajam.com/
http://gigajam.com/guitar/how-you-will-sound/ to hear what students might play at each level

Brilliant Idea 13

Mathletics: bringing a competitive edge to maths learning

MOTIVATING STUDENTS IN maths lessons can be a real challenge. It is also difficult to find programmes which cover a range of topics at different levels. Cotswold Community School is an independent ESBD school catering for boys from Year 4 to Year 11. They have found that Mathletics has raised the profile of maths and produced individualised lessons.

Mathletics is an online resource used by pupils all across the world. It contains hundreds of activities for pupils aged 5–18. There are mental arithmetic challenges and materials linked to concepts and topics from the full KS1–5 national curriculum, ranging from counting and comparing in Year 1 to perimeter area and volume in Year 5 to linear modelling in Year 12.

Elizabeth Moore, Mathematics Co-ordinator, said: 'This programme has totally changed our maths lessons for both our unmotivated and motivated students. We teach boys who have a wide variety of ability and behaviour. The lessons which we set to each boy's own level have made our work so much richer. They can either "learn online" if a teacher is absent or, after a topic is learnt, they can test their own knowledge. Mathletics can even be accessed at home and could provide homework and further evidence.'

There is support at the touch of a button and many teacher-friendly features: all lessons can be printed out; the hard copy shows all the questions; it does the marking too and students can see the correct answers; evidence is named and dated so teachers can see pupil progress very easily.

There is also Live Mathletics, where they compete in mental maths questions with students from other countries (shown on a spinning map of the world). This is especially exciting with the anticipation of which country they will compete with, participating in the 'race' and getting their result. Naturally they are jubilant if they have won but if not, they can immediately try again. All the boys have gained so much confidence from using their own set lessons and Live Mathletics and now they often choose to learn 'on Mathletics please'.

FAQs

1. **Do you need to pay for Mathletics to join in World Maths Day or is there a promotion to encourage schools to join?**

   World Maths Day is a completely free event. Teachers are encouraged to enter their classes and individual students can also enter. Even teachers can participate! Visit www.worldmathsday.com to register yourself or your school. Schools who are already subscribed to Mathletics can sign in with their existing usernames and passwords.

2. **How can I go online and compete with other countries?**

   Students sign into www.worldmathsday.com to play. They will be automatically matched up with students of a similar age and ability from anywhere in the world!

3. **How do you link up with them?**

   World Maths Day is an online platform. Students will be automatically matched with up to three other children when they select to play a game.

4. **Can you print out class certificates or individual certificates for pupils?**

   Yes, every student who takes part will be able to print out a special participation certificate. There will also be special prizes for the top performing schools, classes and students.

Contact and information

www.mathletics.co.uk

Brilliant Idea 14

iMovie supports the curriculum

SOME CHILDREN HAVE very highly developed visual skills. These days they may be exposed to television from an early age and learn more through this medium than via books, radio or even conversation. Some experts claim that YouTube is beginning to challenge Google as a search engine as young people look for information in a visual form.

At Orwell High School in Felixstowe, Food Technology teacher Nick Day was tearing his hair out over his Year 8 group. 'They were really good at the practical work,' he said, 'but they could not write it up.' Often they would just get as far as writing the date and title before inspiration failed. He was interested in using digital video to record progress and showed them how everything worked.

After a quick demonstration, pupils were left to make apple crumble and then they used digital cameras to chronicle each stage of the process before recording a voice-over. The end result is excellent. It includes demonstrations, descriptions of processes as well as an evaluation and it can be used as a resource for future classes. This was their first attempt at working in this way but despite not being familiar with the technology, it took them no longer to make their digital record than it took the rest of the class to write up results on paper. 'This is an important point,' said Nick, 'because if it takes two hours to do then it will be a non-starter in most classrooms but this is an immediate and very direct method of capturing and recording achievements.'

At Frank Wise School in Banbury, iMovie and digital video have become a mainstay of the school's approach to the curriculum, says Head Teacher Sean O'Sullivan: 'We can use it for practice activities which we will not store so children who struggle with speech can have several goes and we can cut the best bits and build a sentence. They can do a voice over anything which gives variety and motivates them to keep trying,' said Sean. 'Using slow motion has been a great way to draw attention to a key point. For example, we might roll a toy car down a slope and then do it again on a rougher surface to show the impact of friction but if a child is looking away the point is lost. We can play it back in slow motion so they really focus on what is on screen.'

He is delighted by the digital literacy of his pupils: 'Although our pupils have learning disabilities, that does not necessarily mean they are slow learners. Sometimes they get stuff really quickly. One boy was editing a clip of himself swimming. It was shorter than the music track he had chosen so he just used copy and paste to make it longer. I was just amazed. It was so intuitive for him.'

You could:

✔ Make a one-minute video for each hour of the school day.

✔ Create a live morning news show.

✔ Record science experiments.

✔ Create a digital record of your local community.

✔ Transfer clips between home and school to help prompt answers to, 'What did you do ...?'

Contacts and information
www.frankwise.oxon.sch.uk/
www.apple.com

Brilliant Idea 15
Choosing wisely

CHILDREN WITH COMPLEX needs might use a touch screen, switches or even eye gaze to access a computer. This often limits the choice of software and resources but schools can now provide a much more varied menu of stimulating activities thanks to ChooseIt! Maker 3. It is an online tool that lets teachers and parents take symbols, photographs, music clips, video, text and sounds and make personalised relevant activities. For example, Leah likes going up and down in the lift. If she clicks on a picture of the lift doors, it brings up a picture of her in her wheelchair in the glass lift in the local shopping centre. This is a good example of cause and effect.

Using exactly the same program, a teacher can put photographs of mini beasts up on screen to see if learners know the difference between a ladybird and a caterpillar. It is just as easy to develop phonics work where pupils match a sound with letters on screen. Teachers can easily make symbol resources as there are over 30,000 symbols and pictures from Widgit Symbols, SymbolStix Symbols and Inclusive Technology's pictures.

Activities can also be downloaded to multiple iPad or Android tablets using the free ChooseIt! Maker 3 App. This means that pupils can try out activities at home, school or on the bus so they are not just confined to one special machine. Schools can keep a record of progression and achievement which is shown in a simple graphical form. They can save or email student achievements and the software and the app both provide a graphic record on completion of each activity so teachers can see how well the children have managed each task.

Pendle View Primary School in Lancashire is a Local Authority special school for children aged between 2 and 11 (nursery to Y6) who have special educational needs. These include moderate, severe, profound and multiple learning difficulties and physical disabilities. Some have autistic spectrum disorders while others have hearing, visual and multisensory impairments.

Jennette Holden, Augmentative and Alternative Communication Leader, likes the fact that ChooseIt! Maker 3 is an open content program which means she can make activities to fit a child's needs. In PE all the children can take part and decide on the activity by clicking on a ChooseIt! Maker 3 grid. She has used it as an assessment tool for visual impairment to see if they can identify different colours and can change the settings so they have white text on a black background. For science she created an assessment grid where pupils had to identify which gadget needed a battery so she could assess knowledge and memory.

The school uses ChooseIt! Maker 3 for registration. Some children press their photograph to register while others can identify and select their name. They also use the program within the sensory room as well as in physical education where pupils select an activity from an on screen menu.

'We have one little boy who finds it extremely difficult to communicate with us. We have used ChooseIt! Maker 3, and we put a photograph into an activity,' said Jennette. 'We soon realised that he was looking very closely at the picture and was obviously interested in it. This was the first time he had shown that level of motivation and attention.'

You could:

- ✔ Make picture making activities.
- ✔ Create cause and effect.
- ✔ Use it for training pupils to use one or two switches.
- ✔ Make quizzes.
- ✔ Create simple multiple choice assessments.
- ✔ Make simple games.

Contact and information
ChooseIt! Maker 3:
   www.chooseitmaker2.com/

Brilliant Idea 16

Radio freedom: make a podcast and take control of the airwaves!

MANY PUPILS HAVE difficulties with speaking and listening. Some pupils are not very articulate and struggle to express their views so they go for simple blunt statements that do not reflect the complexity of their thinking. There are different ways of drawing them out without making them feel they are being singled out for attention.

At Frank Wise School in Banbury, the leavers' class, known as the 10th Family Group, enjoy podcasting every Wednesday morning. One topic they featured was a new scanner at the local hospital. This had been covered by their local paper the *Banbury Guardian* and everyone in the group had recorded a response to the article. Sean O'Sullivan, head teacher at the school, recommends using enhanced podcasting. This lets him put in pupil photos to go with each recording. This is really helpful as it focuses attention and reminds everyone whose contribution they are listening to.

It has also proved to be an excellent choice for mixed ability classes in primary schools. Rebecca Cole, a teacher at Glenaire Primary School in Shipley, answers questions about podcasting:

1. What do you use?
Podium (Lightbox Education). We dabbled with Audacity which is free but Podium does all the sparkly things we need it to do in a much simpler format. We needed something effective AND intuitive and sometimes you have to pay for that!

2. What topics have you covered?
Examples for KS1 included poems and stories from the literacy work and Mother's Day Messages – children recorded a personal message and put the link in their cards (you can hear them now on www.glenaire. bradford.sch.uk).

KS2 recorded a whole class debate on circuses linked to persuasive writing in literacy and a dual language story for our partner school near Paris to listen to. They also interviewed a gentleman who had been an evacuee in the Second World War. The children prepared questions they'd like to ask him and we recorded it. He was over the moon and the children were so engaged and keen to be professional.

We also run a Podcasting Club at lunchtime where children can propose, record, edit and publish news stories. These include topical news, a newsround summary of serious and amusing stories as well as the latest pop/fashion/TV/sport news that appeals to them.

You could make:

✔ A recorded guide for the school.

✔ Interviews.

✔ Stories or collaborative stories (pass the mic around from child to child to carry on the story).

✔ Instructions.

✔ An account of a day trip.

✔ Advertisements and jingles.

✔ Mother's Day messages or any special messages.

✔ A day in... (a different country/ place/era in history/planet).

✔ A Newsround summary.

What are the advantages of podcasting?

1. We try to give children a reason to write, speak and listen by giving them an audience.
2. It's fun – children don't think they're working!
3. Encouraging speaking at a young age encourages confidence.
4. It's interactive and therefore engaging.
5. It embraces new technology – there's no point in trying to fight the technology children use – we need to get on board with them and use it too. They love it – so should we!
6. Parents can enjoy hearing what children are doing without having to wait for parents' evenings and open days.

Contacts and information

www.frankwise.oxon.sch.uk/
www.glenaire.bradford.sch.uk
Makewaves: https://www.makewav.es/

Brilliant Idea 17

Listen and learn with Audio Notetaker

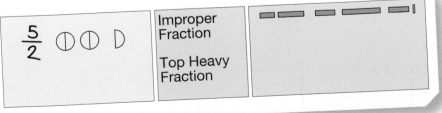

AUDIO NOTETAKER IS an increasingly popular choice for schools and colleges. It is especially useful when working with young people who have dyslexia or other specific learning difficulties who find it hard to listen and take notes in class or from a broadcast.

Audio Notetaker splits a recording up into individual phrases and displays them on screen as a series of bars so it is easy to navigate and find particular points. Then they can colour code information, cut and paste different parts to bring together key points, add their own ideas as voice notes, insert pictures, create a presentation or podcast and use it at home, at school or on the move.

Carol Weale, teaches English at Dane Court Grammar School, Broadstairs, Kent and explains how Audio Notetaker can be used for speaking and listening:

'My Key Stage 3 mixed ability classes are filled with the usual blend of extrovert learners (think out aloud, sometimes very loud!) and the quiet ones who may have written talent but for various reasons find they are unable to shine. I decided to try it out on my Year 8 class, with the focus purely on their listening skills. They were divided into random groups of four or five students and asked to discuss a controversial topic. Each group had a recording device.

'I selected some children to be "spies" and took them aside to brief them about the listening skills that I was monitoring. They had to assess what skills were being displayed, if

any. The "spies" gave feedback to each group who were later informed in the plenary which skills would have earned stars. They were shocked when they realised that they had sabotaged their own scores through poor communication! I showed them the BT "All Talk" videos which show poor and effective group discussions so that they could model their behaviour on that.

'Next lesson, with the spies in place as coaches, they re-recorded another five minute discussion with a follow-up session annotating and scoring their group performance on screen. Vive la difference! Disruptive talk was highlighted in black, turn-taking in blue and going off-task in yellow. The initial test was predictably black but in the second session, it changed dramatically to mainly blue as they referred to the skill bank. Interestingly, they were very aware of asking quieter group members to join in!'

Julie Yaxley is a dyslexia specialist who uses Audio Notetaker as a link between school work and practice at home to help them reinforce new concepts or become familiar with difficult vocabulary. In class she explains new material, gives learners the chance to practise, discuss and absorb new information. At the end of the lesson they create a revision file. Julie writes and records questions. This allows the student to go over the material again and anchor their knowledge by explaining it in their own words.

Together they colour code the recording, so that they can easily identify the question, answer and example. This means that the learners can carry on working at home with confidence, continue to revise and consolidate their new knowledge.

Josh needed helping understanding vocabulary that described fractions. He used a drawing package to write the fraction as a number and draw the associated image. He then imported the image into Audio Notetaker and they discussed the concept. Once Josh was happy with what the fraction represented, he recorded a short summary with help from Julie. This meant he now had a visual and talking alternative to an index card when he needed to revise or check his knowledge.

Advantages of Audio Notetaker

- It is multisensory which helps with learning and memory.
- Students develop better listening skills.
- It provides practice for oracy.
- Students become more confident speakers.
- You can alter the colours so it is easier to read for those learners with visual stress.
- You can save templates.
- It provides an alternative form of revision that is engaging.
- Learners can record in short chunks so they build up information gradually.
- Audio Notetaker helps those with weak auditory memory.
- You can insert pictures and these help students find key points.
- It is easy to edit which means students can learn from their own mistakes and develop editing skills.

You could:

✔ Record audio and edit it visually on screen.

✔ Investigate a topic and record findings and illustrate them. These can then be exported as a video presentation to the class.

✔ Record individual numbers, sounds, shapes or basic vocabulary for EAL or MFL lessons and illustrate them with pictures or imported images.

✔ Listen to a story, segment into chapters and illustrate it with drawn or imported images.

✔ Listen to a debate, speech or factual information and separate the recording into opinions, arguments or speakers. Colour the different contributors.

✔ Record a recipe or set of instructions, divide it into steps and illustrate.

✔ Set a quiz to be answered orally and then record the answers underneath. This would be wonderful for reinforcing language acquisition for a new language or increasing vocabulary.

✔ Record audio directly from YouTube, Truetube or Teachertube and segment or chunk the audio into information, speakers or chapters and paragraphs. Then add text or images to support the audio.

Contact and information
www.sonocent.com/en/buy/

Brilliant Idea 18

Yes, Wii can: turn-taking and getting fit

SCHOOLS ARE TRYING to find ways to combat the growing problem of obesity. Some children have medical conditions which mean they put on weight very easily and it can be hard to find physical activities for children with poor coordination or physical disabilities. The Nintendo Wii is one solution, as Dorin Park School in Cheshire found.

Many people think of the Wii as a hobby to be pursued at home. Others see it as a device targeted at able-bodied people so it might surprise you to know that during the last few years a successful 'Wii-therapy' has been launched in the Peto Institute for children whose motor impairments originate from damage to the central nervous system.

Dorin Park is a specialist SEN college for pupils aged 2–19. They were lucky enough to receive a Wii from MGL, an education and technology support company. Sarah Patchitt is the ICT co-coordinator at the school and was delighted at the prospect of using it to encourage pupils to have a go at bowling. She quickly discovered that it could develop a whole host of skills: physical, social and cognitive.

First of all there are motor skills. Holding a controller and pushing the buttons improves pupils' coordination and fine motor skills while smashing a tennis ball or bowling a ball towards skittles requires full arm movement which helps with gross motor skills. The activities also help with social skills as pupils learn choice making and turn-taking.

Some of the children got very creative making a Wii Mii ('wee me'), an avatar or digitised emblem of a player which represents them in the on-screen world. 'We spent lessons developing their own little characters,' said Sarah. 'It developed their self-image and made them feel very positive. It was fun and raised self-esteem.' The games can also provide opportunities for numeracy as they can count the skittles falling down or work out their score. Pupils find it very motivating and if they are motivated they try harder. In fact, Dorin Park is using the Wii to assess pupils for their P levels.

You could:

✔ Record pupils' pulse rates before and after exertion.

✔ Create a symbol sheet for them to record their feelings.

✔ Use Excel to create charts to interpret that data.

✔ Film some of the pupils using the Wii, script and record a voice over.

✔ Script and record either an audio or video interview.

✔ Schedule a breakfast Wii Fit class at 8:15 in the morning to improve punctuality.

Using the Wii lets students enjoy new experiences: 'They can hold a tennis racquet and hit a ball,' says Sarah. 'In real life they can't.' Not only can pupils enjoy doing these things, she adds, they can enjoy doing them well. 'The pupils are for once competing on a level playing field. I've got a Wii at home but I still can't beat them.'

They say the Wii:

- Improves ability to cope with new tasks and learning new skills.
- Improves non-verbal reasoning skills.
- Helps with cardiovascular fitness.
- Keeps children more mentally and physically active.
- Introduces challenges and risk taking in a controlled environment.
- Improves motor skills balance and coordination.
- Engages those pupils who do not currently enjoy PE.
- Lets pupils set their own challenges
- Works well for pupils who find it hard to follow spoken instructions.

- Is a fun activity and is not seen as physical exercise.
- Can help pupils who are losing mobility in their lower bodies to remain active.
- Helps control obesity.

With thanks to Dan McKeown.

Contact and information
www.teachhub.com/wii-classroom

Brilliant Idea 19

Band identity: music and marketing

WITH PROGRAMMES SUCH as *The Apprentice*, children are familiar with the concept of creating a product and marketing it. It brings together research, planning, writing, collaborating, presenting and evaluation. Even better, there is a host of models for children to draw on so they can move into role play or acting out a part and feel less exposed.

Band in a Box was a 13-week project for Year 6 pupils at Gavinburn School in Dumbarton. It was an exciting and even glamorous project and was so successful that the school is committed to running it every year for the foreseeable future. Head teacher Gillian Penney says: 'This immensely popular project helped pupils to develop their skills. Often those who find conventional literacy activities just reinforce their sense of inadequacy seem to flourish in this activity.'

Year 6 was divided into small mixed ability teams and had a series of tasks to complete. First, they formed a band and allocated roles. They might have been themselves or created an alter ego. Using GarageBand they had to compose a song. They then had to create their marketing materials. Storyboards required pupils to plan and compose, to put forward and justify their creative ideas.

Naturally it was soon time for the band to go on tour so before heading to Europe they had to use the internet to find flights and a suitable hotel. Next they used 'I Can Present', to show off their skills. It is an application designed to bring students' presentations to life by allowing them to create, film and present their work in a new and exciting way using green screen technology. They can film their band or they might choose to create a digital animation.

The children were already familiar with green screen technology as they had used it for other projects such as reporting on an alien landing for *Dr Who* or a live broadcast of a historical event. The more confident talked direct to camera, perhaps having memorised a script or by improvising. Others used the autocue function to stop them from drying up.

Of course, as a highly successful band they couldn't be home in time for the MTV awards so they needed to record their acceptance speech. 'It's amazing how many American accents crept in at this stage,' laughed head teacher Gillian Penny. Finally there are the real awards as the school hosted a black tie, red carpet event with awards for all, from best production to best song.

'Last year we had a boy with such serious learning disabilities that we were not sure if he could stay in mainstream but he took part in every task. He was very active in the French broadcast. For once he could work as an equal partner.'

You could:

✔ Create a product in D&T and run a marketing campaign.

✔ Market a twin town.

✔ Create a series of vodcasts around the school play or sports day.

✔ Think of a fund-raising project and use the ideas to make it a success.

Contacts and information
www.kudlian.net/products/ icanpresent/index.php
www.apple.com/ilife/garageband/

Brilliant Idea 20
The art of the matter

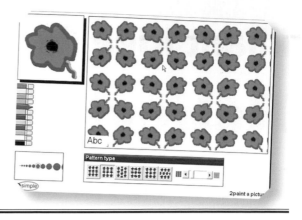

ART IS TACTILE and sensory and that is why so many pupils love it but those very qualities can be a barrier to enjoyment for a minority of learners. There are many lovely art creation websites which allow pupils with poor motor control or sensitivity to textures to take part in creating beautiful images.

The Jackson Pollock website (www.jacksonpollock.org) allows the user to splash paint across a screen. The colour and splodges change every time the mouse is clicked or the finger is repositioned but the pupil does not need to touch, smell or move the paint about with any degree of accuracy.

2Paint a picture is a really easy painting program to use and is especially popular with children in wheelchairs or with very limited movement. The spinner flings electronic paint across a touch sensitive plasma screen or an interactive whiteboard with only one constant touch on the screen. Holly, at a special school in Essex, had very little movement and was in her supportive wheelchair most of the day. By wheeling the chair next to the plasma screen, teachers could enable her hands to touch the surface and colour streamed out from her fingers. She would watch, smiling and laughing as the colours changed and moved.

Marilyn Mitchell, who teaches at Mayfield Special School in Torbay, found that 2Paint and an interactive whiteboard opened up art for many autistic teenagers. Bradley has dyspraxia and finds the mechanics of holding a pencil, charcoal or brush gets in the way of his creativity. Jade does not like getting her hands dirty so the messiness of clay or paint is a stumbling block. Tyler is normally quite obsessive about what he will do on the computer but he did some lovely work with 2Paint. 'We were working on colour themed areas as part of our creative arts/ICT week and we were using green. Initially I encouraged him to touch the IWB using "Splash". I had set it to produce a large pattern to get his visual attention. After just one physical prompt to touch the IWB he experimented in touching different areas to produce a lovely design which we printed. He clearly realised it was his work and was then keen to try other parts of 2Paint.'

For children with a more developed sense of shape and form there are some wonderful websites that enable the user to mimic famous artists. Picasso, Van Gogh and Mondrian websites can all be accessed and children of all abilities can create a picture or diorama in the style of the great masters.

Digital art is something quite unique and really appeals to those children who enjoy watching colours, shapes and textures move in a way that no physical paint can. Bomomo and viscosity merge and draw shapes and colours in a completely new way that is very satisfying to watch. On the iPads there are many wonderful paint apps for children who like to doodle or create while listening or need 'time out' activities. Kaleidoscope and Fingerpaint are examples of absorbing painting apps which can be found on both platforms and are completely free.

Advantages of using painting programs:

- As users begin to explore the package they can produce an original piece of artwork that is good to look at.
- Children who have mental health problems often respond well to colour as it lifts their mood.
- Using even the simplest pattern a strong design can be achieved and seeing a printout of this gives a sense of satisfaction.
- A good, professional outcome can be achieved in a short time. This is particularly advantageous for children with short concentration spans or coordination difficulties.

Websites
www.2simple.com/
www.picassohead.com
www.vangoghmuseum.nl/vgm/index.jsp
www.stephen.com/mondrimat
http://bomomo.com

You could:
✔ Make your own art gallery.
✔ Design your own logo for T-shirts or mugs.
✔ Use created images for reading logs, learning journeys or communication book.
✔ Create wrapping paper, wallpaper designs or posters.

Brilliant Idea 21

Relieving the pressure of examinations

EXAMINATIONS ARE STRESSFUL for most students but for those with dyslexia or other conditions which affect their reading, writing and concentration, the results can be disastrous.

Plans have been announced to make qualifications more rigorous by phasing out coursework and modular learning and returning to traditional end-of-year written exams. When schools heard the news many were worried that the changes to the examination system from 2015 would disadvantage a significant proportion of their learners. According to the Department for Education, 17 per cent of school children have some form of special educational needs such as dyslexia and may have visual difficulties in reading on screen or tracking where they are on the page or screen.

However, the Joint Council for Qualifications (JCQ), has announced a change to regulations that means that literacy software can now be used in exams. The main criteria are that the school can 'prove need' and that the software has been used as a normal method of working for the pupils.

Applications to awarding bodies are made online and your centre should have on file for inspection Form 8, proof of need and the history of provision (what support candidates received in class and assessments); details of the assessments candidates are taking; and diagnostic reports from psychologists and specialist teachers holding a JCQ-approved qualification.

Priestnall School in Stockport has welcomed the change to the JCQ regulations and has found that it has benefited a number of their learners.

The school has 1,300 students aged 11 to 16 years. Twenty-five students in Year 10 required a reader; although not all had dyslexia. Some students had slow processing; others had difficulties comprehending text. There are only 14 teaching assistants (TAs), due to the whole-school approach to inclusion developed over the last decade; so it was not possible to provide a reader for all exams. The SENCO had seen TextHelp's Read and Write Gold in action and thought it could be used as an alternative to a human reader.

Quite a lot of students already had the program. While the school could not provide access in the classroom, they encouraged pupils to use it in the IT suite and at home. Many were using it for homework so it was a familiar way of working. They knew how to set it up and how to work with it. One English teacher was very keen on using it in class and had worked with pupils, encouraging them to use it for essays and other assignments. Some pupils in Year 10 had experience of using it for controlled assessments.

There were a few pupils who did not like it. They would say they could not understand the accent or that the software was reading the text too slowly. They were the students who did not use it regularly and did not know that they had a choice of voices and accents and could change the speed of delivery.

Examinations Officer, Sheila Robson could see the potential of Read and Write Gold and asked the students if they would like to try it out in an examination situation to see if it would be a viable alternative to a human reader. Many of them agreed straight away. 'We decided to use a science paper for our trial,' said Sheila. 'This is one of the hardest subjects to use with a text reader because there is so much specialist vocabulary.'

One of the best things about Read and Write Gold is that you can add extra words so the teacher can build up a specialist vocabulary and change how words are read out. Sometimes text readers work on a phonetic basis and students complain that they do not recognise the word if it is being mispronounced. The teacher can check if the words are spoken correctly and alter pronunciation where necessary. They can also add in technical vocabulary.

Using Read and Write Gold has removed the stigma of needing support in examinations. In the past, students would be in the gym with the TAs. Some students could feel embarrassed. Now they can work in a separate room with headphones and have the text read aloud as many times as they want.

James, a Year 10 student, refused to use Read and Write Gold at first but when he saw how good it was for other students he asked Sheila Robson if he could try it. He was really pleased with the result: 'I wouldn't have been able to concentrate in the gym,' he said. 'I used it a lot more than I thought.'

The school has been delighted with the improvement in grades. Sheila Robson explained: 'We have removed the distractions our learners experienced in exams and have relieved the pressure so now they can show us what they can do. We are now introducing it with our Year 7 English group and feel that it will be very beneficial.'

Hints and tips

- ✔ Pupils need to use it regularly. It has to be a normal way of working. This doesn't mean that pupils have to use it in all lessons but they must use it weekly for homework or in class.

- ✔ Make sure your learners are trained to use the software.

- ✔ TAs and some teaching staff need to provide help, support and encouragement.

- ✔ Involve parents. If they take an interest, pupils seem to make faster progress and be more confident in using the software.

Contact and information

Read&Write Gold: www.texthelp.com/

Brilliant Idea 22

Quite remarkable QR codes on the LearnPad

THE LAST EDITION of *Brilliant Ideas for Using ICT in the Inclusive Classroom* featured a case study from Longwill School for the Deaf in Birmingham which used 'codes' with a PlayStation Portable (PSP), a set of puppets and the popular book *Each Peach Pear Plum*.

In the reception area there are puppets the children have made of Tom Thumb, Bo-Peep, Mother Hubbard and the rest of the crew. On each puppet is a type of barcode which looks like a crossword puzzle. Attached to the table by a low-tech piece of string is a Sony Hold it so the camera scans the code and you will see a child signing the page in British Sign Language (BSL).

It is now quite common to see classroom displays sporting QR codes on a sticker. Quick Response Codes are a type of barcode that can be read using smartphones, some tablets such as LearnPads and dedicated QR reading devices. The code might link to an app, a set of instructions, a brochure or website. They are important in e-commerce but are becoming more prominent in education as they provide a shortcut to sets of materials and 'profiles'.

LearnPads are built on Google's Android operating system. They are robust, safe and easy for staff and pupils to use and bring together all the tools you would expect on a tablet device such as a camera, dictionary and calculator.

LearnPads have the added advantage that they let children access websites and content from publishers such as Education City, Sherston, Yellow Door, Nessy and, unlike iPads, they also work with Flash resources.

A teacher can set up a collection of resources for a class or group of pupils. Year 1 pupils click on a QR code and might be taken to a video clip, a drawing package and information about the Chinese New Year. This means children do not have to go and look for resources or log onto an area on a virtual learning environment (VLE) or go off unsupervised onto the web. Instead, all the information is corralled in one place for them.

QR codes rule

Chris Dunn is the ICT Leader at Grange Primary School in Gloucester. He wanted to raise standards and engage children with special needs and to take technology out of

the IT suite into other classrooms and the school grounds. So far, Chris has bought 60 Quarto (9.7″) LearnPads for class use, plus two Folios (13.3″) for teachers, three large Folio ones for special needs and group work and two Octavos (7.9″) for assessment in the Reception classes.

He likes the way LearnPads can offer different types of support to pupils with special needs. Some children have poor motor skills and some in reception were not able to develop number bonds and did not have a very good attention span working with cubes but the LearnPads increased focus and offered visual and auditory prompts which built up their familiarity with numbers. The instant feedback also made a real difference to their confidence and engagement. 'When children are struggling to get to grips with recognising numbers to 5, 10 and 20 their progress has accelerated because of the LearnPads.'

One of the key features of the LearnPad is the QR Key system. It worked really well for setting up the devices on the network. No more typing in passwords and settings. Instead Chris created a QR Code for the wireless network, scanned it onto the devices and this connected them to the network. This is especially useful for schools looking to roll out one-to-one devices on a large scale as it is a real time saver.

Even when there is no Wi-Fi, teachers can still upload a lesson previously prepared. Codes are printed onto labels and stuck on displays so that they become interactive – as pupils can scan them to get more information. They have also planned to use the LearnPads for a treasure hunt outdoors. By following clues and a site map, children will scan QR codes for word hints and next steps, using the LearnPad at different points. Once they have visited all the sites and gathered all the hidden words they will make them into a sentence which will be the clue to a well-known book.

You could:

✔ Use QR codes to advertise health promotions or bullying or to information that students might be embarrassed to be seen to be copying down.

✔ Link codes to a website, email address or phone number.

✔ Print a QR code on a sticker placed in a textbook to give extra information and perhaps link to a video clip of the author talking about his or her work.

✔ Use QR codes on maths worksheets to link to video tutorials on how to solve the problems.

✔ Create a more realistic class shop by pricing some of the class shop items with QR codes. Children can scan these to find the price in the same way items have a barcode and are scanned at the checkout of a real shop.

✔ Attach QR codes to different bits of a skeleton and link to YouTube videos

✔ Photograph students' artwork and link a PowerPoint to a QR code so you have a virtual art gallery.

✔ Create a survey or questionnaire or let pupils vote for their favourite act.

✔ Put a QR code sticker on a map so pupils on a school trip have access to information in written or audio form and don't have to keep asking 'What's this?' 'What do I do now?'

✔ You might be able to work with your local high street. Put QR codes in shop windows which link to information and images about the premises in years gone by.

Contacts and information
See www.thegrid.org.uk/learning/ict/technologies/handheld/qrcode.shtml#classroom
Create QR codes for websites with www.qrstuff.com/

Brilliant Idea 23

Not just an open book

AMAZON RECENTLY REPORTED that the sale of eBooks has outstripped hardbacks. There is a publishing revolution and the new formats – both eBooks and digital fiction – have advantages for cost-conscious schools and for readers who need a little extra support.

Put simply, eBooks are digital or electronic versions of paper books. Instead of being printed onto paper and bound into books, the text is formatted into a digital file and read via a special eBook Reader. Equally, it can be read on a computer screen, an interactive whiteboard or on a handheld device such as a tablet or mobile phone. The reader 'turns the pages' by using their keyboard or a mouse. Sometimes the text can be read aloud by screen-reading software and the size, style and colour of the text can be changed which makes it easier to see. Digital fiction is more like a video game with elements that can be controlled by the user, or reader. The style will be familiar to gamers and may attract some reluctant readers because it suits those who are more comfortable with 'doing', in this case interacting with the story and activating multimedia elements that support the text.

These new forms of fiction have more than novelty value and are popular alternatives to text-based fiction for disaffected pupils. They are also more accessible than black text on white paper especially for young people who experience visual stress or have eye tracking problems.

Jenny Langley from the Manchester Academy said: 'Initially, we used the I-stars eBooks with lower ability pupils in KS3 as a reward when work was completed. Pupils tend to have an interest in anything that they perceive as unusual so we found this approach really successful in terms of motivation. We then moved on to use them as prompt texts in place of print books for whole-class inference and deduction activities and with small reading groups that we withdraw from mainstream classes. The range of eBooks is fantastic for these groups and we have found them more successful than using print books, especially in paired reading sessions. We think this is due, in part, to the familiarity they feel with technology and partly because they see them as more sophisticated and interesting.'

'In group reading sessions, some of the pupils find it difficult to keep up and their concentration flags as a result; reading from a print text presents a prime opportunity for disengagement. The usual on-task rate is around 70 per cent but when using eBooks we have found the on-task rate to be much higher at around 90 per cent. We attribute this to the fact that learners can read at a pace that they are comfortable with and don't lose concentration as easily. This is especially noticeable in low ability groups.

'For me, the most convincing evidence is that there are more hands up when we ask a question, which I think is due to their increased confidence.'

'I am sure the answer to what is going on is in my nightmares,' thought Matt. 'The Firm is trying to take over the world but what can I do to stop them? If only I could find Jane,' thought Matt. 'She would know what to do.'

Contacts and information
I-stars eBooks: http://istars.education.co.uk/
We Tell Stories: http://wetellstories.co.uk/
Inanimate Alice: www.inanimatealice.com

Benefits of eBooks and digital fiction

They can be used by more than one teacher or pupil at a time which makes them more cost effective and more environmentally friendly.

- The text is never dog-eared or shabby.
- Pupils can highlight parts of the text, for example parts of speech for word work or metaphors. Pupils can bookmark key points to identify a sequence of events or collect evidence for a character study.
- The glossary function in eBooks lets learners look up words and check the meaning in context.
- With digital fiction pupils can use online tools and search engines.
- When working on a text extract, teachers often use photocopied sheets.
- With eBooks an extract can be called up on screen without interrupting the lesson or slowing the pace.
- Schools report advantages especially for children who are poor readers.
- The single page format is better for children with poor eye tracking skills; the ability to change text size is good for some children with visual impairments or dyslexia and the inbuilt dictionary facility is a boon for EAL students.
- The anonymity of eBooks is attractive. No one need know what they are reading and if they are in an environment where reading is not seen as a desirable activity they are not singled out because they could be on a website or playing a game.

The Warwickshire Library Service gets their e-library from Peters, the largest specialist supplier of children's books to libraries in the UK. A group of 15 secondary schools have been involved in a pilot scheme run by the Schools Library Service targeted at KS3 pupils. The schools have access to a virtual library of over 1,200 eBooks which can be read on tablets or smartphones. Students borrow one eBook at a time.

They have found that, contrary to popular belief, teens are not necessarily any more gadget prone than other groups. 'Teenagers have no patience,' said Alice Wyatt, Schools Library Service Adviser, 'and unless the reading platform is really intuitive and easy to use it is a turn off. They needed support to get going and we do need to find other and better ways to remind them of stock they might like. It is not like a physical library where they see the books on the shelves and browse. They have to make a little more effort in an e-library.'

Contact and information

www.risingstars-uk.com

You could:

✔ Use one of the tales from We Tell Stories (www.wetellstories.co.uk/) on an interactive whiteboard for group reading.

✔ Try www.inanimatealice.com. It tells the story of Alice, growing up in the early years of the twenty-first century. The story is written and arranged by Kate Pullinger and the digital artist Chris Joseph. It is a series of episodes with a text-based narrative, supported and enhanced by multimedia components. It uses a combination of text, sound, images and games to weave an interactive story of Alice. The reader goes on a journey through her life from the age of eight through to her 20s.

✔ Look at and create https://twitter.com/twitterfiction, 140 characters or less.

✔ Read a book together and start a class blog or wiki (see Brilliant Idea 13).

Brilliant Idea 24

Twitter brings in virtual visitors

MANY PEOPLE THINK of Twitter as a way of keeping abreast of celebrity news or as a medium for publicising their own achievements. In fact Twitter can be a real boon for schools. It can help in three different ways:

- for training and updating staff knowledge;
- to form a virtual community; and
- as a tool for classroom learning.

Emma Chandler was an early adopter of Twitter. She tried it out in the classroom when she was still a PGCE student and found that it let pupils work in quite different ways. She wanted to link pupils with outside experts in real time; it was almost like having a visitor in the room, albeit a virtual one.

Emma joined #Ukedchat: 'Every Thursday morning they have discussions on different topics and this professional network is a great source for ideas and expertise.' She found that it connected her to a very knowledgeable community. Teachers can post a query and get a response from others who have gone down the same route. There are also Twitter events when a group comes together to discuss particular issues or topics.

Tracy Playle is a social media expert and has her own communication consultancy called Pickle Jar Communications. Her advice to schools is that they should stop creating volumes of content and instead start conversations and curate content for others to make sense of. 'Look at what happens at the school gates and the kind of conversations that take place there and replicate these in your tweets.'

Instead of bombarding people with details of Ofsted inspections look at things they can buy into: three ways to help your children make good friendships, 10 places to park the car near school. Show pictures of an art display and link to a post on your school website about Art without the Mess. Tweet five spellings for a class and link to a website on how to help children learn how to remember spellings.

Hints for making the best of Twitter

✔ Use established hashtags which let you keep track of conversations. The following are useful for classroom networking: #ukedchat; #teacherontwitter; #classtweets; #education; #edtech; #teaching.

✔ Click '@Mentions' to see if any followers have replied to any of your 'tweets'.

✔ Go to #Discover to find people or organisations to follow. Many companies, celebrities, and non-profit organisations use Twitter, ranging from Stephen Fry (@stephenfry) to Greenpeace (@greenpeace).

✔ Review the Tweet Media and Privacy settings. These are listed under the Account tab of your settings. Check the applicable boxes and hit Save.

Twitter as a classroom tool

Pupils can be slow to commit to new media and many like to lurk for a while which can be frustrating for teachers who are keen to embrace the new technology. Emma Chandler's classes started by creating paper tweets and posting them on a physical wall. This helped them get the idea of the brevity and immediacy as well as learning some of the Twitter conventions.

Emma has used Twitter simply as a medium to send out messages such as letting her group know about new seating plans. She has also used it as a stimulus to class discussion, posting a picture on Twitter and giving pupils 24 hours to think about it and come up with a response. Next she started to use a Private Network (PLN) with a closed account so only a very few people could access it. In the early days Emma had two teachers from other schools who engaged in debates about the role of film in society. Then, when her pupils were more confident and could use hashtags and the other features of Twitter, they went live.

A Year 8 class was examining the work of a MP in Citizenship. Instead of relying on Wikipedia or textbooks, they tweeted MPs from both sides of the House. The class was surprised that MPs would respond to them in real time via tweets and that they could ask questions and receive answers. They asked them how they had become MPs, how they communicated with constituents and what had been the busiest time they had experienced since taking office. Emma has used the same approach to work on bullying and to find out about different charities and their campaigning work.

When pupils see responses to their tweets, they begin to realise that they are part of an online community. Now she finds her pupils are quoting tweets in their citizenship essays and are working directly with real, up-to-date evidence. This means they have to weigh up facts for themselves, sift fact from opinion and develop judgement instead of relying on received opinions. Emma was lucky that she had some notable early successes which encouraged pupils and senior management to take it seriously: 'It took a while to develop the classroom model but replies from people such as Boris Johnson and the BBC really got everyone behind it as a concept. Being retweeted by a charity or the BBC gives pupils a buzz which is like no other. It is very real.'

The language of Twitter

- Tweet – a Twitter single update of 140 characters or less.
- Retweet or 'RT' – forwarding a tweet from someone else so that all of your followers can see it.
- Trending Topics (TTs) – topical subjects which many users are tweeting about.
- Lists – users can link people or organisations which are related in some way, e.g. charities.
- Hashtags – prefacing a word with a '#' will create a hashtag, a kind of keyword which is searchable.

Contacts and information

www.picklejarcommunications.com/
www.theguardian.com/teacher-network/teacher-blog/2013/oct/21/
    best-citizenship-lesson-tnews-riots-digital-natives

Brilliant Idea 25

High-tech hide and seek

'**T**URNING ON WI-FI** will improve location accuracy' we are told and for geocaching it is especially important to know where you are and where you are going.

Geocaching is a treasure hunt with technology. It can be played indoors, in the school grounds or at a park or outdoors centre. The idea is to hide containers called geocaches at different 'waypoints' and then send out teams armed with GPS devices to track them down. You can make the adventures harder by adding in challenges for pupils to complete or give them clues to solve a mystery. You can link geocaching to just about any curriculum area.

James Langley works for Bradford Metropolitan Borough Council and has become something of an expert in this area. He was inspired by the work of a Canadian teacher Jen Deyenberg when she was working in Scotland and now he and Education Bradford's Curriculum ICT team are developing geocaching projects in schools and across Local Area Partnerships.

The first step is to decide which devices to use. You can buy specialist devices but some schools may prefer to download a Geocaching App for iPhone or Android. The next step is to practise setting out a trail with waypoints where the caches will be hidden. You want to make sure that the hiding places are not in a direct line of vision for other groups as this spoils the 'hunt' element. James Langley recommends: 'Set out your caches with the odd numbered caches on one side of the grounds and the even on the other side. This way the children travel further during the lesson when they are following the route in numerical order.'

In Bradford they have enjoyed many different geocaching activities. One of the first was at East Morton Primary School. The trail involved a series of eight hidden boxes around the grounds of the school with questions and information linked to the theme of 'Chocolate'. Head teacher Louise Dale found that the activity developed many different skills including teamwork, perseverance, problem solving, speaking and listening.

There have been many different examples since those early days. One school found QR codes in their caches which, when scanned, brought up questions about Ghana:

- In which continent is Ghana situated?
- Can you find it in an atlas and can you name the countries it is sandwiched between?
- The Ghanaian flag combines four different colours. Can you find out what the flag looks like and make your own version?

In another school they dressed up as superheroes – even the staff – and put their knowledge to the test with some tricky questions:

Question 3. Which superpower does Superman NOT possess?
1. Magic Hex
2. Superbreath
3. Flight
4. Super strength

Question 6. Batman protects what city?
1. Chicago
2. Metropolis
3. Gotham City
4. New York City

Access is a major issue for pupils with physical disabilities as the terrain needs to be fairly flat with no hazards. Many schools get round this problem by using their outdoor classroom or school grounds for geocaching events. Others may like to go further afield. One of the great advantages is that pupils get a lot of exercise without realising it. This is why it is an activity that never loses its appeal, especially for those learners who are easily distracted and those who find it uncomfortable to sit in a classroom for any length of time.

Many secondary schools are running transition summer schools for their new Year 7 pupils. Parkside School wanted a geocaching day based on the Olympics. The team arrived early to set up 10 hidden 'caches', each containing a multiple choice question based on the Olympics. Each of the answers corresponded to a code. Once pupils had all the codes they could open a digital safe which contained two more challenges. They had to make a one-minute video explaining geocaching and complete a real geocaching route around the local village of Cullingworth.

'The GPS devices we use track how far the pupils have travelled in a day,' said James. 'By the end of the day we had travelled a total of 10.2km whilst having fun in the sun.'

Suggestion from Jen Deyenberg

We had comics hidden in the caches. They had to find the six panes of the comics and put them in order, I had some which were text based, some which were just images so we had to put things in order based on text clues and visual clues.

The organisation of geocaching groups is always important to the success of the activity. Make sure you label the caches (A–F in this case) and send groups to different caches to start with to spread them out. Each person in the group has a role. In this case the roles were recorder (with a clipboard), navigator (with the GPS), cache opener and replacer, photographer, and clue collector (don't lose them!). These responsibilities assure that each person gets a role and that all aspects of the activity are monitored, on track and recorded.

You could:

✔ Write a short story divided into eight parts. Pupils have to collect, reorder and reconstruct the narrative.

✔ Create a tour of your school building. Each cache will contain an interesting fact. This works well for a transition project.

✔ Produce a quiz about your city or local area. The groups have to find all the questions and then use a search engine or reference books to check their answers.

Contacts and information

@jdeyenberg; www.trailsoptional.com
www.geocaching.com/live/default.aspx

Brilliant Idea 26

Coping with chaos in the classroom

Oh no, there is a wasp.

COPING WITH CHAOS is a story-based program targeted at children with emotional and behavioural difficulties. It features a child called Sam, who finds himself in a variety of difficult situations which are commonplace for most students. Rosie Murphy of Fairfield School explains how she used the program.

'Initially, I set up the program on the Interactive Plasma Screen to use with a group of KS3 students. Some of these students have emotional problems, some are on the autistic spectrum. The program has three levels of difficulty ranging from simple to more complex emotions. When the program starts we are introduced to Sam and he waves hello – a great touch as confirmed by my students, who enthusiastically waved back!

'The program features a variety of easily recognisable locations for the students to choose from but, to avoid confusion, only two are shown on the screen at a time. Once the location has been selected something surprising happens to Sam and he expresses an emotional reaction. As one of the options, students can choose which surprise they would like Sam to receive. This is a useful tool as they can select a familiar situation, for example dropping an ice cream on the floor. At each stage in the program there is an animation of Sam and the students are unable to move to the next stage until it finishes so it encourages them to pay attention to what is happening on screen.

'Although Coping With Chaos works very well with students who can access the plasma screen by touching it, I also used the switch option with a group of KS3/4 students. The program can be accessed by either one or two switches but, to accommodate all the needs of the students in the group, the mouse or touchscreen can still be used at the same time. Once the correct scan rate is set for the individual student they can access the program by pressing a switch when the scan box reaches the required button.

'As each story is completed I can give out a star and the student can print out a certificate giving their score. There are signs and symbols in the program (sadly not PCS) and my students watch and sign in response. Throughout the program there is also positive reinforcement of the correct way to behave and simple explanations on why certain choices might not be appropriate. The program promoted a lot of discussion with some students and we talked about different reactions to difficult situations and what is appropriate behaviour.

'I printed off the pictures in the "resources" section of the program. These let students look at the choices and think about the options before they made their selection using a switch. This meant they did not have to choose, scan and use the switch all at the same time. There are also sheets for lotto boards and dominoes as well as large and small pictures of the emotions with empty speech bubbles so words can be added.

'Overall this program was a big hit with our students. The graphics are clear and interesting. The subject matter is appropriate and it lends itself to group work on the Interactive Plasma Screen.'

You could:

- ✔ Use the program on an interactive whiteboard.
- ✔ Match pictures and symbols for different emotions.
- ✔ Use a digital camera to take pictures of pupils to illustrate different emotions.
- ✔ Type different emotions into Google and click on Images.
- ✔ Talk about different situations or use social stories.
- ✔ Discuss what is appropriate behaviour and how we can decide what to do in difficult circumstances.

Contact and information
Coping With Chaos:
   www.inclusive.co.uk

Brilliant Idea 27

No need to blow it up

MAISIE IS **12** years old and is in Year 8 at a comprehensive school in Harrow. She has rod cone dystrophy, nystagmus and a squint which means that she needs to have size 24 text and has to hold the page very close to her face if she is to decipher print or illustrations. Worksheets have been a real problem because they spread onto adjoining desks, fill up her school bag and she has to sort through piles of crumpled paper to find what she needs. Now, with help from her form teacher and head of Computing Gavin Calnan, Maisie is using an iPad to access information.

What can an iPad do?

iPads have inbuilt accessibility options which are found in Settings. Go to – General – Accessibility. Voice Over, Invert Colours and Zoom are the most useful for a visually impaired user. Voice Over reads whatever is on the screen. Gavin has set it up so it has pitch and does not sound like a robot: 'What I find really good about this feature is how clear the voice is and how easy it is to understand. You can control the speaking rate from very slow to very fast and the students I have worked with have no issue understanding the voice.' Zoom allows the student to zoom into anywhere on the screen and enlarge objects by 100 per cent up to 500 per cent and works in any app. Invert Colours produces light colours on a dark background which many users find easier to see. Other useful apps include Siri for voice recognition which lets users dictate text, emails, notes and even use it to enter search terms into a browser.

What works for Maisie?

Maisie frequently uses the camera to take pictures of worksheets and then zooms in. This works very well with the Invert Colours accessibility option so when she takes a picture of a worksheet, an object in science or a page from a textbook, she can invert the colours on the screen so she has white text or a white image on a black background. This lets her see the resource better.

Using iBooks means she can access English literature texts which can be set up with a large font. Gavin has also uploaded Maisie's homework diary onto the iPad through iBooks and she uses Pages to take notes, edit her diary and complete worksheets which can then be emailed or printed out. She has an email account so she can send her work directly to teachers. The app FileBrowser lets her access documents on the school network, including teacher resources such as PowerPoints and worksheets.

At first Maisie was not sure about using an iPad but after some training she became more confident and has found that she now has better access to the curriculum. Many of her friends have iPads at home so if she runs into trouble they can sometimes help her out but, even better, she can show them things she has found on the internet. The iPad means she is able to be part of the class and work at a much faster pace.

Website
http://appadvice.com/applist_ipad_client_view/apps-for-the-visually-impaired

Brilliant Idea 28

Creating a communication-friendly environment with symbols

WARWICKSHIRE AND FIFE local authorities have taken symbols out of special education and put them into mainstream schools. Both authorities are using symbols to support children who find language and print a problem and to develop differentiated materials.

Fife County Council advocate using Picture Communication Symbols (PCS) throughout mainstream settings. The pilot project has used Boardmaker Plus! from Mayer-Johnson to provide a consistent communication-friendly environment. It started with 11 primary schools and has grown to 104 primary schools across Fife, and is now beginning to move into secondary.

Sandra Miller, head teacher at the Fife Assessment Centre for Communication through Technology (FACCT), explained: 'The transition from primary to secondary can be very stressful for some pupils. We have used symbols to let pupils share their worries and fears. Symbols can support pupils' communication, and also their organisational skills and recall. It can help them to access text and improve their ability to cope with change, so you can see why we hope that more schools will adopt symbols!'

Contacts and information

Why we use symbols: Independence – www.symbolsinclusionproject.org/symbols/why_symbols/independence.htm

Widgit – www.widgit.com/

FACCT – www.acipscotland.org.uk/facct.html

Mayer-Johnson: testimonials – www.mayer-johnson.co.uk/whole-school-testimonials

Boardmaker Case Study – Fife Assessment Centre for Communication Through Technology

www.youtube.com/watch?v=Hg_xy0wOPuU&feature=mfu_in_order&list=UL

The project has made an impact. Already many secondary schools are 'symbolising' their public areas and individual teachers have received training so they now understand why symbols might be effective and can see ways they could use them in their classroom.

'Once schools are on board,' said Sandra Miller, 'they take ownership for developing symbol support and resources. This means that they can intervene and make immediate provision for a child rather than waiting for a speech and language assistant to make them two weeks later, as sometimes happened.'

Maureen Pickering, Deputy Headteacher at Benarty Primary School in Fife, said, 'If children have any kind of learning need then symbols are the way forward. Schools can customise symbols for their own environment and they are so easy to use that the children can make their own visual timetables. Learners are using symbols from an early age and are quite used to this and the staff find the symbolising is quite addictive!'

In Warwickshire they have been using Widgit Literacy Symbols. Pauline Winter at Clapham Terrace Primary used symbol versions of 'Roman' books with a boy, who was very difficult to motivate and a girl who was Portuguese with huge gaps in English vocabulary.

'The boy loved the symbol book,' said Pauline. 'I read the first page, then he wanted to read the rest. When I paused to check the vocabulary, he became impatient and said, "Let's get on. I want to read this bit." In the second session that week both children showed continued interest, and remembered a few of the new terms introduced. In this session they used the flash cards to identify specific vocabulary and discuss the meanings. By the second week, both children had a good recall of vocabulary and good attention to the tasks. They both made a big effort to recall the labels from last time. The specific vocabulary they could recall was Rome, Emperor, sword, shield, aqueduct, legion and the purpose of turtle formation.

'By the end of that week they were able to read from the symbol-supported books. These books have symbol pictures linked to the new and difficult vocabulary. It was clear that the symbols helped them to remember and understand the concepts.'

Key points for symbol support:

✔ Teachers may not want to symbolise every word. They might just use them for key words or difficult concepts.

✔ Symbols can give a voice to children who have speech language and communication needs (SLCN).

✔ They can help children understand a text so they have a context for decoding words.

✔ They can help with choice making activities.

✔ Teachers can build a bank of differentiated resources.

✔ Verbal instructions can be reinforced with a symbol card.

✔ They can help pupils be more independent.

Brilliant Idea 29

Visualiser brings classwork into focus

ONE PIECE OF technology that can help pupils with visual impairment or dyslexia and works well for students who aren't even in school: the visualiser, a camera-come-projector capable of high-resolution output. Helen Davis (Science AST) shows how the visualiser is transforming life for teachers at Davison C of E High School for Girls in Worthing.

'Before we had visualisers it was very hard work providing differentiation and meeting the needs of different pupils: large print and a special font for Natalie who has a visual impairment, photocopying handouts onto yellow paper for Beth who has specific learning difficulties (SpLD). Photocopying took up too much time and cost the school a lot of money. We also had to incorporate lots of repetition in class for children who had problems concentrating and any girl who missed a lesson would have to catch up by working from books and handouts and talking to a friend. It is a very different story now.

'Science involves a fair number of demonstrations. In the past we would have had a group of girls standing in a circle round the front table. There would be lots of jostling; some would not be able to see clearly what was going on and others would walk away and soon forget the steps they had to follow to replicate the experiment. Now we use the camera on the visualiser to film what we are doing during the demonstration so it is large enough for all to see on the whiteboard screen and play it back during the practical so everyone can see what comes next. We can also keep recordings for revision and pupils enjoy making their own videos using stop frame animation. This helps them model conceptually difficult ideas and share them with a wider audience, making a richer learning experience for all.

'The visualiser is a wonderful tool for enlarging detailed processes. With circuit boards in design and technology, pupils need to see exactly where to apply a soldering iron but the components of a circuit board are very small. With the visualiser, we are not just helping girls to get things right, we are also keeping them safe.

'Another example is the investigation into factors affecting the rate of photosynthesis, utilising aquatic plants. All green plants take carbon dioxide in and turn it into oxygen in their leaves. The key way we can measure this easily in class is to count the number of oxygen bubbles produced from a cut plant shoot in a set time period. We use Cabomba, a fluffy pond weed for the aquarium which works very effectively even with very low light levels. Often the bubbles are so small that they are hard to see with the naked eye. Now that with the visualiser they are larger and much more obvious we can also record the evidence. We know everyone is seeing the same thing now which makes for more reliability and precision.

Contacts and information

Visualiser forum:
   www.visualiserforum.co.uk/
Inclusion case studies:
   www.visualiserforum.co.uk/
   case-studies/sen/
AverVision: www.avermedia-europe.com/
   default.aspx
Elmo: www.elmo-visualiser.co.uk
GeneeWorld: www.geneeworld.com/
Samsung: www.samsungpresenter.com/
WolfVision: www.wolfvision.com/wolf/
   1.shtml

You could:

✔ Play 'Kim's Game' with a range of objects or flashcards – really simple, but great for recalling vocabulary (during MFL lessons, for example).

✔ Most visualisers allow you to do basic stop frame animation to watch change such as ice melting or basic story making.

'The visualiser helps us to meet individual needs within the classroom. We can put a handout on the visualiser and put a yellow acetate over the top so Beth can see it clearly. She is not being singled out and it does not affect the others in the class. We also have learners who have a good grasp of science but cannot write up their work. We can assess how much they know by letting them make posters or record them presenting to a group. This is very useful for peer- and self-assessment. We can also put up a good written account on the visualiser from one of the other pupils so they have a model of what they should be aiming at. Sometimes they need to see what "good work" looks like in order to improve their own work.

'Hayley has ASD and has problems interpreting pictures as do some of the girls with specific learning difficulties. Somehow they cannot see a two-dimensional image on a page and relate it to something three-dimensional. When we study the differences between plant and animal cells we make cardboard models and show them on the visualiser. Somehow working in 3D lets them see the differences so much more clearly and there is less room for misinterpretation.

'Because visualisers are so widely used in school lessons, we are building a bank of videos and this can be very useful when children are absent from school for long periods or who are school refusers. The children have to do some practical assessments as part of their GCSE and we give them a run through so they know what to expect.

'Aisha was in hospital having operations on her knees when we did an investigation on force and momentum. We ran a model car down slopes taking very precise readings via a light gate. Instead of getting her to work from a book or copy up a friend's notes, we videoed the lesson and emailed it to her in hospital so she could understand exactly what we had done. Now she can do the paper knowing full well what is required and she has as good a chance as any of the girls who were physically present in the lesson.'

Top ten tips

1. Ensure that staff and pupils are already comfortable with the existing display technology in the school (like interactive whiteboards).

2. Consider buying a visualiser with its own light source (these are more versatile – but they cost more). Nearly all of these have light source inbuilt these days!

3. Make time to see the technology being used. Try visiting a school that already uses the technology, or ask to have training from the education consultant for the company.

4. Ask if the images/videos created by the visualiser can be shared easily. Usually, they can be saved on a laptop, on the interactive whiteboard or on a SD memory card. (This is not worth it, nearly all visualisers do this!)

5. Skill the children up. The visualiser you choose needs to be robust enough for everyday use – but it will last longer when everyone knows what they are doing!

6. Consider buying a docking station – it will allow you to shift from laptop to DVD to visualiser seamlessly.

7. Spend a little time planning when you will use your visualiser over the year (spontaneity is also good!).

8. Pair staff who are ICT literate with those who are less so to ensure consistent use within the school. Encourage teachers to share their ideas and teaching techniques (use the Visualiser forum).

9. Visualisers are like any other ICT resource. To get the most out of them, you need a plan. Used properly, visualisers mean the advantages we were promised with interactive whiteboards (increased pupil engagement, reduced preparation time, improved results) are finally realised.

10. To ensure visualisers don't just clutter your desk, you have to get the children on board. Once they have shared their work, interests and ideas on the visualiser, they won't let you forget about using it!

Brilliant Idea 30

Using a TomTom to make sense of the world

K.C. KELLY-MARKWICK IS head of ICT at Oakwood Court College in Devon and her work with Global Positioning Systems (GPS) won her the Handheld Learning Award for Special Needs and Inclusion 2010. This project could easily be adapted to different groups of learners in schools and helps with mobility and communication skills.

Oakwood Court College is a specialist residential educational college for 35 students with Asperger's syndrome, autism, Down's syndrome, Williams syndrome and other types of learning difficulties. Self-reliance is a key quality that the college fosters in its learners to ensure that people with learning difficulties have the knowledge and confidence to apply for jobs and live as independently as possible when they leave college.

One project focused on a comparison of the speeds of email and conventional 'snail mail'. Students started by making their own Christmas cards on the computer and printing out a copy. They wrote the name and address – and most importantly – the postcode of the person they were sending it to on the envelope. Staff at the college explained what a postcode is and what it does. To help this process they visited the website Flash Earth and put the postcode into the satellite navigation system to see how it related to the location and postcode. A screen grab of the map was printed out and used as evidence in their folder (OCR National Skills Profile Module 1: Interact and use ICT for a purpose).

Once the students understood how the postcode works, they moved on to using the TomTom GPS system. With a bit of help from staff, the students put in the postcode for their local post office and set off on foot to find it. There they bought their stamps and posted their cards. When they arrived back at the college, the students had to send the same card to the same person via email. The students then compared how long each took to arrive.

'People think of the TomTom as a technology just for motorists,' said KC, 'but it has been an inspiration, giving the students greater independence and improving their communication skills. It led them to go into the local community and use maps and life skills that they may not ordinarily use within a college environment.'

'These days there is a greater choice of technology to help people find their way. Now students arrive at Oakwood with their own iPad so they can stay in touch with friends and family back home. I soon realised that they were confident users and so I decided to find ways to integrate different apps into their life skills work so we

You could:

✔ Compare maps – printed ones, Google Earth, Google Maps.

✔ Go for a walk with cameras and clipboards – take pictures and create your own map.

✔ Look at Google Maps' Street View.

used Grid Player for communication with a non-verbal learner and the Change4Life Smart Recipes app for healthy eating was used in a shopping and meal prep session. We also uploaded the Google Maps app to help the students find different locations in the local community. It is our hope that by teaching our students to use their iPads for something other than games and YouTube that we are introducing accessible transferable skills that they can use when they leave Oakwood Court College.'

The satellite navigation system has been used for other outside visits so the students have started to learn about different places within their community. It also links to modules such as the OCR for Accreditation Life and Living (ALL) where they look at the use of technology in everyday life, at college and work. As they go out and about they can find out about:

'The students get a greater sense of purpose from these activities,' said KC, 'and their whole experience has been enriched as a result, developing their education and practical skills.'

1. CCTV cameras in the shops.
2. ATM bank machines.
3. Control panels at pelican crossings.
4. Shop counter check-out points.
5. Public pay phones.

Contacts and information

Flash Earth: www.flashearth.com/
Apps: https://itunes.apple.com/

Brilliant Idea 31

Get the monsters reading

Teaching synthetic phonics can be fun when it has a story element

Teach Your Monster to Read: First Steps and Fun with Words are free online games from the Usborne Foundation to help children practise and consolidate the essential first stages of reading. Teach Your Monster to Read features two voices familiar to many children. There is Simon Farnaby from BBC's *Horrible Histories* and Mr Thorne from *Mr Thorne does Phonics*.

The children also enjoy the story elements which are part of the software. They know that the monster has crashed his spaceship in a strange land. He cannot read his handbook and needs to rebuild his craft and fly home. The program encourages them to design their very own monster which they take on the journey with them. This part of the process may take some time as the children decide on a name and personal characteristics such as size, colour and what it likes to eat.

Snowsfields Primary School in Bermondsey is a one form entry school with 232 on the roll. A growing number of children have English as an Additional Language. Matt Rogers, ICT Subject Leader, used Teach Your Monster to Read with Year 1. It gave them a chance to engage in large scale art as they made giant monsters in the classroom from tissue paper. They worked together in groups using language to describe what they were doing and many of the children enjoyed the practical element. The monster also featured in mathematics sessions when they planned a party for the monster, working out what to buy and measuring out ingredients. They made him a castle using mathematical shapes and in the summer term they also grew some plants for him to enjoy.

But the main aim of the software was to help the children build their knowledge of phonics. Teach Your Monster to Read starts with initial sounds and builds up step by step. Listen to a sound, match it to a graphic, blend sounds, segment words in a sentence.

The Usborne Foundation program works well for recording and reporting. Staff can click on a child's name and see when he identified the sound correctly, the percentage of time he got it right and compare to all the other children in the class. This means that even very shy children who hesitate to join in group activities can show what they can do. 'I can track progress, identify the sounds individuals are having problems with – or the ones they are really good at – and use the data to pick out sounds we need to go over with the whole class.'

While there are many phonics programs on the market and others are used in Snowsfields School, Teach Your Monster to Read seems to boost children's progress. Matt believes this is partly because it appeals to different learning styles with its strong visual and kinaesthetic

Questions to ask yourself:

✔ Will the program save you time?

✔ Will it be engaging?

✔ Does it have good support materials?

✔ Is there an online community using it so you can exchange ideas?

✔ Will children get bored with it or does it grow with them?

✔ Can you collect and collate data from it?

✔ Does it work well for whole class as well as individual work?

elements. Anya, who started during the school year, could not manage simple consonant–vowel–-consonant words but within a few sessions she could decode words and construct simple captions in the program.

It works well for children with special needs too. The school has Rainbow Class, a resource base where children with special needs have some of their lessons and receive extra support, joining their main class for certain parts of the week. Bertie has autism. He is 'non-verbal'. Mostly he works one-to-one with an adult and even then he speaks very rarely. However, with Teach Your Monster to Read the teachers have evidence that he is developing knowledge of phonics. 'It would be hard to assess his progress since we can't hear him segment words or blend sounds,' said Matt. 'With the game we can see he is moving on.'

Matt has a number of tips for other schools. He believes that there is no single program which works for all children so make sure you have a variety of phonics resources. Social media is a good way of finding out what other schools are using and he advises teachers to check what the people they follow are using. Above all, try before you buy. Download a program and play it to see if it works for your learners and make sure the pupils have an opportunity to have a say because, 'There's no point planning to use it if they don't like it.'

A longer version of this article was originally published as 'Monster idea for phonics', in *Primary Teacher Update*, Vol. 01, Iss. 27, December 2013, pp. 50–51, www.primaryteacherupdate.co.uk. This extract is reproduced by kind permission of the publishers MA Education.

Contacts and information

www.teachyourmonstertoread.com/accounts/sign_up
http://blog.teachyourmonstertoread.com/

Brilliant Idea 32
Memory matters

MEMORY IS THE basis of all learning. Anyone who has worked with a child who has been in a road traffic accident or is experiencing memory loss after chemotherapy knows how slow progress can be and the sense of frustration shared by the pupil and the teacher. Here is a bright child who is suddenly groping for words, finds it difficult to think about two things at once and gets 'overloaded' very quickly.

Rachel Lewis is Assistant Director or Learning Support at Darwen Aldridge Community Academy (DACA): 'Ryan was the first child we had with really obvious memory problems. When he came to us in Year 7 he could not remember a single significant life event, not the birth of younger brothers and sisters, birthdays, trips out. In fact his problem was so severe that his parents arranged for a brain scan but there was no obvious cause for his problems.'

ICT can be a very effective medium for young people like Ryan. Some children can be put off their stride by noticing mannerisms, clothing, accent or intonation or trying to gauge the other person's mood. A computer is always the same and that can be very comforting for children who have a history of bad relationships with adults. Equally importantly, once children have their headphones on, they tend to become engrossed and are less likely to be distracted by the behaviour of other children so concentration is more absolute.

While working with pupils who had severe memory problems like Ryan, Rachel was also aware that working memory was a problem for many pupils and was holding them back in all subjects. The school decided to make it a major focus for student support. They used Mastering Memory from CALSC. Unlike other software interventions, Mastering Memory is a teaching program where a helper works with the pupil to ensure that the memory strategies transfer to the classroom and real-life situations.

Staff had INSET on memory training and started to use memory games as starters for lessons. They also encouraged children to create mnemonics for recall, to be 'active readers' using a highlighter to pick out key terms, to create a glossary and draw visual cues to learn and reinforce new vocabulary. Some adapted the old game of 'I went to the market and bought…' so it was relevant to different curriculum subjects to help pupils recall information from previous lessons.

A Higher Level Teaching Assistant withdrew some children for up to 20 minutes at a time to work on Mastering Memory. In Ryan's case it had a dramatic effect. After two terms his memory improved so much that he could follow lessons more easily and was better behaved and much more communicative.

Jane Mitchell, a former speech and language therapist and creator of Mastering Memory, has some suggestions for classroom strategies to help relieve the pressure on children's memory:

1. Show And Tell: give them an overview before the lesson starts, explaining what you want them to learn and how it will be tested later.
2. Make it visual: use mind mapping, a topic web, grid or diagram.
3. Pre-teach vocabulary: don't let them get distracted wondering what words mean. Check they can say words, know what they mean and can spell them.
4. Play Pictionary with curriculum vocabulary.
5. Focus their attention: highlight important points with colour.
6. Explain clearly: adapt your language if necessary, pause between sections, chunk the information.
7. Write it up: put key words and numbers on the board.
8. Help the child to record information: keep copying to a minimum. Hand out transcripts, use cloze activities, photocopy notes. Make notes easier to follow: colour code alternate lines on the board, let learners make an audio recording of the lesson or take a picture of the board with a mobile phone or iPad.
9. Remind the learners of memory techniques: suggest strategies such as saying it aloud, drawing pictures, visualising and creating videos in the mind.
    Talk it over: ask pupils to tell someone what they learned, recall the three most important facts from the last lesson or make up quiz questions for other class members.
10. Reflect: ask them what was easy to remember and why.

A longer version of this article was originally published as 'How to boost your pupils' memory skills' in *SecEd*, 5 September 2013, www.sec-ed.co.uk/. This extract is reproduced by kind permission of the publishers MA Education.

Contact and information
www.masteringmemory.co.uk/

Brilliant Idea 33

Making school app-propriate

APPS ARE FAR too difficult for children to write themselves! The creators of the education movement called Apps for Good certainly don't agree and the high quality of entries in last year's Apps for Good awards prove the point. Apps for Good is an open-source technology education movement that partners with educators in schools and learning centres to work with young people 10–18 years of age.

Rodrigo Baggio, the founder of Apps for Good, says, 'Our goal is to transform the way technology is taught in schools; to empower students from all backgrounds to seize the opportunities of our digital age and create solutions to the problems they care about, using technology. We want to build a new global generation of problem solvers and makers: students who can create, launch and market new products that change the world. We believe that technology can be a great equaliser and a massive force for good to transform lives and communities around the world.'

But how does the rhetoric translate into classroom practice? So how can we enable pupils to create apps for this next generation of technology? Kudlian has come up

with a solution. They have liaised with AppFurnace to give schools a free trial so students can create their own apps. AppFurnace is available for free from the AppFurnace website to trial and users only pay on publication. The interface is drag and drop with ready-made widgets to enable students to write and compose their own apps and preview them via the AppFurnace Player on their own phones prior to publishing.

Three pupils from Cockburn School in Leeds created The Story Wall app. They identified that it was not often possible to become 'creative' in a certain lesson time and when they were working under pressure they would get frustrated and experience that feeling of 'hitting a wall'. They wanted to help people to write at a time that was right for them and that they could collaborate with anyone else during this time to compose not just a good story, but a great one!

This app puts constraints on the amount of words each participant writes before handing it on to a selected friend to continue the story.

'Not only are students learning to code and create a useful app for their friends,' said James Betts, Managing Director of Kudlian, 'but they have to work collaboratively to produce the end result. We have had a group of students from a pupil referral unit who have found terrific satisfaction from working together to produce something that they are proud of. They created help apps for games they were interested in as well as a guide to their PRU.'

You could:

✔ Make an app to guide pupils through course content complete with QR codes to identify appropriate websites.

✔ Make an information app with recipes or directions.

✔ Make an identification and visual timetable app for students who need to know who is visiting them and who they are.

✔ Create an app with favourite videos or music for individual pupils.

Websites

www.appsforgood.org

www.kudlian.net/

Brilliant Idea 34

Money, money, money

FROM SEPTEMBER 2014 financial literacy will be a compulsory element of mathematics and citizenship for secondary pupils and there will soon be a plethora of games, apps, websites, video case studies and simulations to support the new curriculum.

The world of money is changing. It's no longer a cash economy with pay packets and cheque books. Now finance is online – from shopping to banking and above all entering into contracts. Children are becoming involved with money at a younger age through mobile phone contracts, downloading apps and ring tones and buying online.

Jess has dyspraxia and dyscalculia. As a result she finds it difficult to handle cash and paperwork and packing bags at a supermarket checkout is very difficult for her. She gets round many of the problems using the web. She recently found out about the charity MyBnk through Twitter and approached them to deliver a workshop for her dyspraxia support network called Dyspraxic Me. They worked on a module called Living Independently which covered attitudes towards money, steps after moving in, reading bills, household costs.

Jess gets information about special offers via her mail box and can take her time to work out if the discounts are useful or just hype. She likes online shopping and sees that in the future when she leaves home it will be a useful way

of getting her groceries. She also finds online banking is a better way of tracking her money than working through paper based statements as she can use the search facility to check different transactions.

These days there is considerable concern about the levels of student debt young people in Higher Education incur but they are the fortunate ones as they usually have supportive parents who have some financial security and when they leave university they have reasonable job prospects. The real problem lies with more vulnerable young people who might have poor budgeting skills and come from families with debts and money problems.

pfeg is a financial education charity which organises My Money Week each year. They advise on resources and have been responsible for some very successful training. Barton Moss Secure Care Centre in Manchester said, 'The overwhelming response from the staff present was that this was a vital area for the pupils they teach in order that they have the best chance to re-engage in society and not to re-offend.' A social worker at Hartlepool Borough Council reported: 'directly as a result of using the resources two young people now intend to complain about the harassment they have been receiving from pay day loan companies.'

Many young people who pass through the care system might be living independently from the age of 16 and be an easy target for loan sharks and payday lenders. Many Looked After Children will have an Individual Savings Account with a £2,000 contribution from the government which will probably be the largest nest egg they receive in their lives.

Alan Brown, deputy head of Kingsmead School, a Pupil Referral Unit in Derby, tries to make sure that money and life skills are woven into as many areas of the curriculum as possible because the pupils respond well to anything which is practical and which will help them in their future life.

One group planned a BBQ for 25 pupils plus staff. As well as deciding on the menu and making shopping lists, they looked at shopping online and in store. They found that computer shoppers could easily get carried away because they did not see a trolley filling up but that they could easily edit an order, deleting items or opting for cheaper brands to fit their budget. They used a spreadsheet to compare the cost of paying for their shopping by cash, credit card or via a pay day loan. They were shocked at how much extra they might pay especially as some lenders charge a late repayment fee of £100.

'Television is full of adverts for loans and it is important that students understand the implications,' said Alan Brown. 'Our Looked After Children will move into independent living when they are 16 and be responsible for their own budgeting so we need to prepare them for that.'

Packed Lunches			
43 packets of crisps	at 29 p each	will cost	£12.47
4 bottles of cola	at 47 p each	will cost	£1.88
2 apples	at 38 p each	will cost	£0.76
4 packets of starburst	at 30 p each	will cost	£1.20
6 cheese sandwiches	at 55 p each	will cost	£3.30
7 Penguin biscuits	at 17 p each	will cost	£1.19
Altogether I will spend ⟹			£20.80

Contacts and information

Credit action: www.creditaction.org.uk
Pfeg: www.pfeg.org/planning-teaching/introduction-what-financial-education
MyBnk: http://mybnk.org/
Money Saving Expert: www.moneysavingexpert.com/
www.leeds.gov.uk/c/Pages/TakeAStand/default.aspx
dyscalculator – an app for those with dyscalculia: www.dyscalculator.com/
dyspraxic.me.uk

Brilliant Idea 35

Resounding success: audio in the inclusive classroom

Carol Allen, Advisory Teacher for ICT and Special Needs in North Tyneside

Carol has been an 'early adapter' of every form of technology, ensuring it meets the needs of children with disabilities and learning difficulties. Here she talks about ways of exploiting sound in the inclusive classroom.

'One of my "mostest fav" bit of small-scale kit at the moment is the Sound Shuffle from TTS. Small, neat enough to fit in my bag when travelling from school to school and cheap enough to recommend to others, it has so many uses that it has become one of my "essentials"! It is able to take up to four minutes total recording time and then these can be replayed either sequentially or randomly.

'I am currently fascinated by using sound in the "inclusive classroom". Now this can be clever, with podcasting and complex multimedia productions, or instant and simple. In an EYFS classroom that I am currently working with, we are looking at how embedding technology within the learning environment, in addition to the teaching and learning activities, can make it accepted practice rather than a "special" event or add-on to the main life of the classroom.

'The shuffle comes with wall attachments making it ideal for adding sound or voice to wall displays; imagine young children describing their pictures and why they created them as part of an art display – how much better than their name and year group? By using two shuffles they could each choose another's work to comment on so adding peer assessment at a very early stage in an entirely appropriate format.

'In the reading corner, selected books have shuffles next to them with audio recordings of the stories so that non-readers, and/or those with language barriers or print impairments can enjoy reading independently. These can also be sent home to support families who want to read with their children, but who also have difficulties doing so. As it is so quick to record a story, these can be changed easily to keep the engagement high.

'Meanwhile, in the storytelling hut in the outside learning area another shuffle offers a random selection of story starters, such as a character idea, a sound effect or a snippet of music. Children can take it in turns to press and then "tell" a story using the stimulus that they hear. After lunch it has been quickly re-programmed to give items to be located for a "treasure hunt", such as a stone, a leaf or a stick.

'Most EYFS classrooms offer a wealth of activities and teaching areas to choose from. For Harry the range of choice was overwhelming and so he always made the same choice and was reluctant to try new things. His teacher set up a selection of activities on the shuffle, including his favourite, playing randomly. He could press, listen and move to try unfamiliar activities independently. As the top of the shuffle can be removed and a photograph or symbol fixed underneath, activities can be identified clearly. Equally, tactile items could be fixed to the lid and a selection of their "properties" recorded by the children – the opportunities are endless! Well worth a try – why not have a go and see what you can do?'

You could:

✔ Use it to make up the recorded sound clips from a story by asking pupils to find the correct character from a selection of puppets or toys.

✔ Record a series of instructions to be completed by the child.

✔ Record a series of story sequences to match scanned pictures from a book, in sequence and then jumbled up for the child to put in order.

✔ Have a series of pictures for the child to record their own story.

✔ Record a simple story book for the child to follow while looking at the book.

✔ Record objects that a child has to find (ideal for playtimes).

✔ Record a 'consequences' style story for each child in a group to add their own element and then illustrate the completed story.

✔ Make a series of activities for children to do in PE or free choice time.

✔ Record children's reactions to a visit, stimulus such as a picture or texture to create a word bank of 'wow' words.

Contacts and information

Information and suppliers: www.r-e-m.co.uk
www.tts-group.co.uk

Brilliant Idea 36

Dawn of the machines

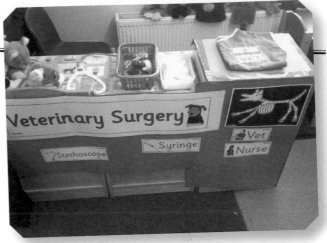

DAWN HALLYBONE IS a well-known name in the world of educational gaming. A recent convert to consoles and PSPs, she is ICT Coordinator at Oakdale Junior School in the London Borough of Redbridge and a founder member of the Redbridge Games Network. She won the Hand Held Learning 2009 Special Achievement Awards. Here she talks about the power of games:

'Children play games all the time. We learn through play when we are babies. So many social skills and rules for behaviour are learnt in the playground but that all goes when we move into school. I wasn't a gamer till three years ago. I didn't own a console and when my daughter, then aged six, asked for a Nintendo DS I said no.'

But then Dawn heard about the Consolarium project in Scotland, which was bringing computer games into the classroom. This project had shown that games could help pupils develop self-reliance, problem-solving and critical thinking skills and create shared social contexts where learners could relate better to others.

Dawn introduced 30 Nintendo DS Lites into the school and found that pupils and teachers quickly became more ICT confident and more ICT literate. They discussed problems and issues together and children who had consoles at home shared their expertise with teachers and others in the class. It also led to lots of writing. The school set up a blog where the children wrote about the games they were playing at home. They also designed their own games, wrote reviews and made films about the games. They didn't just play: they worked very hard too!

Games also give us an insight into children's skills. Pupils with special needs often have low-level reading skills and are judged on that, but in fact they may have sophisticated thinking skills which we never uncover by conventional means. They may well have a high degree of media literacy and it is up to us as professionals to engage that through play. Games can provide a visual stimulus for writing. Take the Land of Me, which is just beautiful. It is an old style picture book, brought to life in a different way; pupils respond to the graphics and we can use this as the basis for communication at all different levels.

Games can bring in a good element of competition. This is not the sort of competition where pupils with special needs compete against others and constantly come last but where they strive to better their own performance. For example, with Word Coach they are competing against themselves, trying to improve their spelling scores. Doing Dr Kawashima's maths on a Nintendo beats pen and paper activities hands down and it certainly encourages speed and mental agility.

For many children with dyspraxia or physical disabilities, the (Nintendo) Wii can bring a new dimension to physiotherapy. Instead of being singled out to leave the classroom, they can play on Wii Fit with a friend for 15 minutes and do their exercises in a fun way.

Good teachers use good tools and games can be very good tools indeed.

Games across the curriculum

Alissa Chesters, ICT Coordinator, has been using games with children at Oakdale Infants School. Nintendogs is a game where children look after virtual dogs. They have to feed the dog and can take him to the park, buy toys, teach him commands such as 'sit' or 'stay'. All this takes place in an online world and children use the Nintendo DS screen and a microphone. They choose a name for their dog at the beginning of the game and call their dog via the microphone. They might play on their own with the dog or link up other players using a wireless linkup. The game has an internal clock and calendar so if they don't feed and exercise their dog regularly, they see the consequences.

The school developed lesson plans and a topic web and the game was the catalyst for work in many areas of the curriculum. They had to keep the Nintendogs diary up to date so they spent at least 10–15 minutes writing each day for literacy. For non-fiction they wrote up a day in the life of a RSPCA officer. They had a video of Crufts and themed their sports day as crufts4kids. In D&T they had to design a kennel and for science they looked at what they needed to look after their dog and to keep it healthy.

You could:

- ✔ Use games to inspire pupils to better their own scores and keep a chart to record improvement.

- ✔ Use a bank of carefully chosen games or technologies as an overlearning or repetition tool.

- ✔ Ask pupils to record on a sound shuffle or Easi-Speak mic the rules to their games for others to follow.

- ✔ Make a database of good games for pupils to search through and find the appropriate resource.

- ✔ Make posters about their favourite game.

- ✔ Use games as a stimulus for writing, i.e. create a life for your Nintendog.

Remember

1. Games enable teachers to see what the learner can do.
2. Find teachers in other schools and piggyback off their expertise.
3. Share resources and ideas.
4. With games the teacher is not in charge: some children will know more so you need an environment where it is acceptable to share knowledge.
5. Do not confine the use of games to 'golden time'.
6. Look at ways of using games on interactive whiteboards as the basis of whole class activities.

Contacts and information

Trailblazers recognised at
Handheld Awards: http://tinyurl.com/652kf9b
Consolarium:
    www.ltscotland.org.uk/usingglowandict/gamesbasedlearning/consolarium.asp
FutureLab:
    www.ltscotland.org.uk/Images/futurelabgames_and_learning_tcm4-452087.pdf

Lights, action, sing karaoke?

KARAOKE MACHINES HAVE been around for a long time but now there are a range of relatively cheap children's karaoke machines and packs to use on the computer that can be projected onto a bigger screen to enable groups of children to access them. Music and singing are a great way to overcome speech and language difficulties, including stammering.

Studies show that early musical training physically develops the left side of the brain, which is responsible for language and reasoning, and research carried out by the Centre for the Use of Research and Evidence in Education claims that singing contributes to children's health and well-being, their learning across the curriculum, language development and overall confidence.

Nathan Cresswell of Pioneer School in Basildon listed the numerous ways in which singing to a karaoke machine helped those children who otherwise found it difficult to communicate.

'We have used karaoke as a way to encourage confidence, listening and performance skills, especially for those who choose not to speak for a variety of reasons,' he said. 'These can range from elective mutes to crippling shyness. We have also found that singing along to a familiar song helps stammerers and those with enunciation difficulties.'

Nathan chose to use a karaoke pack on the computer linked to an overhead projector to allow children to deliver and perform songs in assemblies as well as special events.

'We found that the correct microphone was essential to the success of the delivery. The lapel microphones or head mics (Madonna mics) allowed students to focus on the highlighted words and concentrate on the performance rather than the hand-held microphones, which tend to get in the way of what we were trying to achieve.'

He often uses music and singing at the beginning or end of a session but stresses that good visuals and clear text are very important, as is the colour of the highlighter that pinpoints the words being sung.

'We had a young lad called Paul who was 14 and had chosen not to speak. He really couldn't see any need to voice any requests and consequently found it difficult to enunciate any essential requests that he might have. Paul loved our karaoke sessions and would light up when the time came to sing along with everyone else. It really gave

You could:

✔ Sing your favourite songs at the end of the day.

✔ Hold your own 'X-Factor' or 'The Voice'.

✔ Hold your own karaoke disco.

✔ Practise favourite songs for delivery in assemblies or school productions.

✔ Make up your own pantomime including the songs.

✔ Just have fun!

him a purpose to speak and sing and he obviously enjoyed the activity. His favourite selection was Beatles songs!'

As well as the benefits gained from using their voices and practising hard-to-pronounce vocabulary, other side benefits came from an increase of confidence, self-esteem and the social skills needed to take turns. Singing often brings joy not only to those taking part but also to those listening – it takes the stress away from essential speech therapy practice and injects a wonderful sense of fun.

For a price of around £15 for a karaoke pack this is a fantastic tool for all children.

Extra information

Stand-alone karaoke machines for children start at about £50: www.argos.com

Karaoke packs for use on your computer start at about £15: www.argos.com

Just Dance on the Wii contains an element of karaoke along with dance moves for £15: www.amazon.co.uk

Sing to the world is a karaoke website where, for a subscription of £6.99 per month, you can get unlimited access to a huge database of songs: www.singtotheworld.com

Sing Up (www.singup.org/) is a membership scheme which helps schools with resources and a framework of achievement as they become 'Singing Schools'.

Brilliant Idea 38

Accessible music in a cube

YOU MAY NOT have heard of the Skoog yet, but you soon will. It is a white squeezy cube with colourful curved discs on five sides which let very severely disabled children make music for themselves. Usually musical notes are dictated by the size and shape of the instrument which makes them. A recorder needs to be hollow and have holes which can be covered up to change the pitch but the Skoog lets children play 12 instruments including the piano, flute, guitar, drums and marimba. More than that, it can be programmed with any sampled sound, a song, a sound effect or will launch a midi device or a program such as GarageBand.

Pioneered at Edinburgh University with experts in music, physics and psychology working together, it can be configured to suit individual needs. It can be made sensitive to the slightest touch to encourage children to engage in cause and effect activities. The Skoog acts as a sensor and links to software which does all the hard work of making music so children who do not have the physical dexterity to play a guitar, who cannot control their breathing to play a flute, can still make music for themselves.

They have been trialling it with children who have severe disabilities including sight loss. Rhys is four and a half and has nystagmus, photophobia, autism and global developmental delay. It worked well for his hand and eye coordination and his gross motor skills. In fact, he played the Skoog with hands, feet, knees, elbows, head and chin. He also crawled through the play tunnel while playing it and ventured up the climbing frame. He expressed his opinions and told us that the instruments he preferred were the drums, guitars, xylophone, drag n' drop playthrough and sampler. Staff reported that he played for a very long time (unusual for him) and showed unexpected inventiveness, using various parts of his body to make music.

Cameron is the same age as Rhys and has a similar range of disabilities. His hand/eye coordination was good enough to control the Skoog easily, so staff turned the sensitivity down to make it more of a challenge for him. He loved hearing different instruments and realised he could make long notes rather than short ones. Usually Cameron has a very short attention span and he did walk away twice but chose to come back and try again. Staff were very impressed with how long he played with the

Other uses:

✔ The instrumental service in Orkney is using the Skoog for instrumental tuition.

✔ At SENS Scotland, the Skoog supports inclusive music making for a wide range of ages and abilities.

✔ Use the sampling functions and sound effects for storytelling.

✔ Fife's Digital Literacy Creativity Team has used the Skoog for digital soundtrack music.

Contacts and information
www.skoogmusic.com/
Use YouTube to find videos

Skoog and he certainly had lots of fun.

Brilliant Idea 39

A Word to the Wize

PUPILS IN THE sixth form at Oak Field School and Sports College in Nottingham have been making computer games. Many schools have been quick to embrace the challenges of the new Computing curriculum but Oak Field is a school for children aged 3–19 years with severe and profound learning difficulties and/or physical difficulties and they are using a very new piece of technology called the WizeFloor.

Imagine an enormous iPad on a floor where children can jump, lie, shuffle, or roll across it in a wheelchair and you begin to see some of the potential of this interactive floor. It works on shadows not on touch and can be used by several children at the same time so it encourages interaction and collaboration.

The system consists of a ceiling mounted projector, a Kinect camera, a 4 × 3m reflective vinyl floor mat, a set of audio speakers, plus an Apple Mac mini. The pack also has a bundle of software and templates so teachers have some ready-made activities and a set of tools for making their own games.

Katy Wilkinson is ICT coordinator at the school and worked with the sixth form evaluating and designing games. They compared games on the WizeFloor with ones they had seen on games consoles, iPads and desktop machines to identify the things that were important. They decided that music, characters and images were key features.

On the WizeFloor they looked at jigsaw games, matching pairs activities and a cause and effect game where they jumped on balloons. They had to decide which they liked best. One of the most popular was a simple flower game. As students move across the floor a chain of flowers follows them, creating melodies as they appear. They might also choose to try to jump on some large ladybirds which scuttle away, making shrieking noises. Great fun!

The games had an impact on many students. Greg had such poor coordination that he had problems going up and down stairs. After trying the pairs game he realised that by walking he could make things happen. Soon he started to focus on planting his feet and stamping and was much more aware of different parts of his body.

Jamie has very limited movements so adult helpers put him in the middle of the WizeFloor and held a muslin cloth above his head. As he moved his head, he could see the flowers projected above him.

The group decided to make some games for younger children in the school. One group went out and took pictures on the iPad to make a matching pairs game for orienteering. Jigsaw games worked well too because as pupils worked together to rebuild the image there was lots of communication. 'Many of them were arguing and discussing,' said Katy. 'Telling each other where to stand and which square they should choose. Their skills for collaborating and communicating were much more developed because they didn't see it as work.'

Because of the range of disabilities at Oak Field School, staff regularly use photo evidence and e-portfolios. Katy was keen to use the WizeFloor in the same way so in their review period on a Friday afternoon she started to project photographs of different things they had done in the week such as learning to clean their teeth or making soup. The WizeFloor became a focus for identifying what they knew, what they remembered and as a stimulus for purposeful discussion and peer review.

The school has tried different types of interactive technology in the past. 'One size does not fit all,' says Katy. 'We use a lot of iPads in the school but they are not so good for those who struggle with a small screen and for those who have problems with fine motor skills. Those pupils need something bigger where they can use gross motor skills and be much more physical and the WizeFloor is ideal for them.'

Benefits of the WizeFloor

- It is good for kinaesthetic learners.
- It can be used for curriculum focused activities.
- Multiple users can play simultaneously.
- Use it for games making.
- It is an excellent device for cause and effect activities.
- Children learn through play.
- It promotes communication and collaboration.
- It encourages concentration and close attention to visual stimuli.
- It offers 'Cloud' storage and collaborative tools for teachers.

Contact and information
www.wizefloor.com/

Brilliant Idea 40

Writing in code

CHILDREN AS YOUNG as five are learning simple programming. The move was part of a government reform of the National Curriculum and is a welcome attempt to move children on from being consumers to being creators of technology.

By the end of Key Stage one, pupils should be able to create and debug simple programs as well as 'use technology safely and respectfully'. They will also be taught to understand what algorithms are and their function in programming.

As well as helping them to develop skills which might be in demand in the world of work when they leave school, programming and apps creation has other educational benefits. Research by the Consolarium project in Scotland has shown that games making can help pupils develop self-reliance, problem solving and critical thinking skills.

Clare Dibble is a class teacher at Oakdale Junior School in Redbridge. She has a Year 1 class with 17 boys and nine girls including one child who has visual impairment and learning difficulties. Clare describes herself as 'not a natural coder'. Like many teachers she was apprehensive at first because coding is such a new area with specialist terminology such as predicted outcomes, algorithms and variables. She did try Scratch when she was training but didn't really understand it.

Fortunately companies such as Espresso and Rising Stars have taken the pain out of the new requirements and devised units which contain all the instructions and support

materials a teacher could need. Clare had seen the We Are Programmers module in Rising Stars Switched on ICT and was keen to have a go with this.

The class spent a lesson discussing what made a good animation. Many of the children enjoy cartoons, the stop frame animation of *Wallace and Gromit* and could talk knowledgeably about the Lego movie which had just come out. They learned that, although the end products may look very different, all animations start with a storyboard.

There were certain constraints the children had to bear in mind. Their animations had to be very simple with just three frames, each one featuring the same background.

In their second lesson the children used the Paint tools in Scratch. The icons were very familiar to them as they are used to using 2Simple software so they could transfer the skills they already had and knew how to copy and paste.

Next they looked at the Hour of Code website and had a play with the algorithms for the Angry Birds. 'There was lots of new language and new vocabulary here,' said Clare. 'We decided to keep it simple so they were playing with algorithms, rather than creating them. It also made me more confident about using Scratch tools and I could come up with better suggestions for things they might like to try.'

In their next lesson, they created a background and their sprites. Often they used very simple figures or animals. One of the best was the figure of a footballer with a picture of the stand as a background. The animation showed the footballer scoring a goal. Interestingly, this was created by a girl who had no interest at all in the sport.

The coding activity was successful with a wide range of pupils. Some children loved the fact that they were spending a whole lesson drawing pictures. Children new to English liked the fact that it was such a visual activity with easy instructions.

The class worked in pairs, which was a good strategy because they were not all at the same level in literacy but had complementary skills. 'I took an idea from the Hour of Code to make one child the navigator and the other the driver and swapping every ten minutes so it wasn't always one child doing the work with the other child as an onlooker.'

Hints and tips

- Remember that many primary pupils already play computer games – on consoles, PCs or mobile devices. Tap into that enthusiasm. You are moving them from playing to creating games.
- Break the class into groups of two and three and pooling their skills and knowledge. Some children are good at art while others have a logical mind.
- Think about the way you can use these activities to teach teams.
- Link computing to other areas of the curriculum where possible.

Contacts and information

www.risingstars-uk.com/all-series/
    switched-on-computing/?offset=all
www.espressocoding.co.uk/espresso/
    coding/whatisit.html
https://code.org/educate/hoc

Brilliant Idea 41

The crazy gerbil

AT **WESTFIELD ARTS** College in Weymouth, they use ICT across the curriculum to make their children as independent as possible. 'I want our pupils to be actively engaged in using a whole range of software to create their own animations, videos and learning resources,' said Yvonne Aylott, head of ICT. 'If they can't actually write things they can record their voice, they can make videos or take photographs. ICT can be very liberating and motivating. It lets us meet the same learning objectives in different ways which the children find more accessible.'

The school caters for pupils with moderate learning difficulties, many of whom have autism and/or complex needs and also supports pupils in a number of mainstream schools across Dorset. Two pieces of software have been especially good for their learners. Voki is a free online service that lets you make your very own talking avatar and Crazy Talk a facial animation program which will animate any photo or image so that the lips move and the character appears to speak a typed script or recorded voice.

Year 9 pupils were working on self portraits. They chose photographs of themselves or did drawings and used them as models for Crazy Talk. Once the face is loaded into the program they decide what they want their character to say: 'I was drawn by James. He found it hard to do my eyes,' 'I think my ears look big in this picture'. If they prefer, they can record their speech and attach it to the character. 'It is surprisingly realistic,' said Yvonne, 'because even when the character is not speaking, they are moving and there is a certain amount of noise (background animation), as if they are just pausing for breath. It is quite motivating for our learners. We had one boy who did not speak willingly but was really trying to make some noise so that his self portrait would not be silent. This project was good because it let the pupils think and talk about what they had done whereas they would find it hard to write an evaluation.' The pupils have found some creative uses for the software. They have made some talking trees and when they were having school council elections they animated a cow pat who did a rousing speech along the lines of, 'Vote for me. I'm so soft and squidgy!'

With Voki the children select a background such as a city at night or a harbour, choose a character, change the hair and features, add some accessories such as moustaches and sunglasses, type in some text or record a message and the character speaks. 'We used this to create some jingles for a charity campaign,' said Yvonne. 'We had an Elvis type avatar and it was just so easy to create.'

Using animated faces is obviously great fun but Yvonne warns that it is important to have some structure not just play around with it, 'The technology is not that important, it is the uses we make of it that matter. We did some work using photos of the class gerbil and then recorded a script so that the gerbil spoke and told people what it needed: 'I need clean water,' 'I like something to chew.' Children with autism can have problems with empathy but when children are devising their script, they are in fact thinking about that other person or animal and that is a good first step to thinking about others' feelings.'

You could:

✔ Animate products to create adverts.

✔ Have animated talking faces at the top of a worksheet to explain the task.

✔ Use animated talking objects to explain a history topic such as how to make a mummy.

✔ Make speaking and listening tasks to be followed by the children.

✔ Make speaking faces or objects to be included in school webpages.

✔ Create a play with a series of talking characters. This is a great way to introduce spoken versus written language and play script format.

✔ Make a storyboard for a film or story and create characters ready to animate. Look at www.creaturecomforts.tv/uk/ for some trailers and ideas for creating animations.

✔ Ask children to record and animate their thoughts on some artwork, book, poem, play or television programme and leave on the IWB for pupils to listen to.

Contacts and information
www.voki.com/
www.reallusion.com/crazytalk/
http://blabberize.com/

Brilliant Idea 42

Poetry pleases thanks to Clicker 6

A TALKING WORD processor might not be the obvious choice for a poetry lesson but in Northamptonshire they have found that it can make pupils more critical and discerning when they are being creative.

Becky Ludlow teaches at Moulton Primary School in Northamptonshire. She has 32 children in her Year 4 class with a very wide ability range. Some are working at Year 2 level and some at Year 6. Some children have dyslexia, others have autism or significant problems with working memory and one or two have problems controlling their behaviour and emotions.

Becky was introduced to Clicker 6 and could immediately see the point of it. Here was a literacy tool which could work for pupils learning English as an Additional Language, those with restricted literacy skills and above all pupils who lacked motivation and confidence. Becky is one of a growing number of teachers with dyslexia. She struggled all through school and was

assessed and diagnosed at university where she was given Dragon Naturally Speaking. This transformed her life and enabled her to cope with the pressures of written work so she is very clear about the power of technology to support those who struggle with reading and writing.

She introduced Clicker 6 to her classroom and was surprised at the difference it made, not just to those who needed writing support but also to her gifted and talented group as well.

The class was working on poetry. They began with a poem called 'Four Voices' and although they managed to read the poem it was quite lifeless. She split them into groups and each group had to work out ways of enlivening their delivery for an audience, using voice and gesture. 'They sometimes forget that poetry is not about words on a page but is also a performance,' said Becky.

As Bonfire Night approached they got out the black paper and chalks and made shape poems based on the idea of fireworks. This led into work on similes, metaphors and

You could:

✔ Create poetry activities with a Clicker set to support the targeted vocabulary.

✔ Copy and paste a Shakespeare text or information from a specialist website to support a topic.

✔ Use the alphabetical Clicker set format to encourage personal vocabulary building. All sets can be saved and opened by individuals to support and carry forward their learning.

✔ Insert images, drawings and videos to bring e-books to life.

✔ Record audio files straight into the Clicker Book to enhance the writing process.

✔ Use the predictor function to extend the written work and then read it back to ensure fluency.

✔ Explore all the open ended writing frames.

✔ Go on to Learning Grids (www.learninggrids.com/uk/) to find a bank of great resources.

thinking about the sounds of words. Becky found some poems on the internet about fireworks and created some worksheets with the opening part of a simile, 'As fast as …'. Then she wrote the endings and they had to come up with the first part. With less able pupils she looked at similes which they might incorporate into their writing.

Clicker 6 really came into its own when they wrote their poems. Ellie rarely used full stops but because Clicker 6 will only read the sentence aloud when you hit the full stop, she focused more on what she was writing. She started to think and to write in sentences so, instead of producing a stream of text, her writing began to be more precise and to have a structure. Becky was also very impressed with the effect of Clicker 6 on the more able group: 'Often they do not do much editing,' said Becky. 'They write a large amount and their work is very creative. Using Clicker 6 meant that their work was read back to them and they could think about manipulating the text, restructuring and creating more complex sentences and improving the tone. As a result they were working on much higher writing level skills.

The class worked in small groups, reading out one another's poetry, providing praise and suggestions for improvement. The children enjoyed the activities and Becky found that Clicker 6 engaged her pupils, helped her differentiate her lessons and provided support at all levels.

Contacts and information

www.cricksoft.com/uk/
www.tagxedo.com/

Brilliant Idea 43

Making the news when you are four!

STUDENT TEACHER **M**ATT Fenn was asked to support young children's writing in his teaching practice, but how do you get four-year-olds to compose more complex sentences? After all, most of them will be still working at letter level and composition is a very laborious process.

Matt decided to use an iPad at his placement school, in Essex, to see if the children could make use of the video facility to structure their composition. He asked a group of four-year-olds to watch a video of him going to the local dentist. They talked about what they had seen and listed the order in which things happened in Matt's video. They were then asked to make their own television programme in groups of three. One child would be the interviewer, one the interviewee and the third would be the cameraman with the iPad. The interviewers were placed behind a cut out cardboard box to make them look as if they were on the television. 'The children really became involved with the activity and it gave them a way of reflecting and revising their work,' Matt observed, 'and the fact that they had a format made the task easier for them to achieve a really effective result.'

As they explored further, the children were able to use the microphone icon next to the space bar on the iPad to speak and to see their own words appear on the screen. This is such a useful tool because it means that the iPad becomes a flexible recording device as well as an excellent note taking tool for anyone who finds writing difficult.

The children couldn't wait to display their work to the class, to other school staff and to parents and were confident in explaining their composition techniques. An added advantage was that the teachers and parents could review and accurately assess where the children were in their understanding of information.

Matt soon found opportunities to let everyone display their prowess in using connectives, adverbs and adjectives when a guide dog visited during the next week. 'I was really not sure that the children would be able to achieve the results that they did, especially the children with very poor attention span and abilities,' Matt said afterwards, 'but the results were amazing, especially when we reviewed the transcripts of the children's videos. They really understood the learning and enjoyed using the video to show what they could do.'

You could:

✔ Video interviews for an electronic book.

✔ Video a story enacted by pupils or narrated whilst videoing in the school or grounds.

✔ Video instructions or 'how to' videos when cooking or making models.

✔ Read or recite a song or poem and fit a video to the words.

Website

mashable.com/2013/06/05/video-edit-apps

Brilliant Idea 44

Using online video to bring citizenship to life

PUPILS ARE ACCUSTOMED to using social networking websites and modern technologies such as digital cameras. They expect to see these technologies in the world around them but even now the majority of school resources are paper based. Online video is a good choice for promoting debate in PSHE, RE & Citizenship.

Andrea Keightley is an ICT teacher at Montsaye Community College in Northamptonshire and is a fan of TrueTube. 'The resources that are currently available on TrueTube are specifically aimed at the age group I need them for. The video clips are presented in a modern, snappy way that appeals to teenagers of all abilities. They use real people that the audience can identify with, and present a much needed, reliable replacement for out-of-date resources that often represent an unrealistic picture of society today.'

Students are suddenly willing to engage with the lesson as they can relate to the people on the screen. Some of the topics covered in the Citizenship/PSHE curriculum are 'difficult' subjects to teach. They entail exploring issues that may have affected students in the class. TrueTube is an online collection of resources, covering everything from bullying to obesity, from street crime to sexual promiscuity. Headlines reflect the variety and impact of the resources: 'Slept With 2,000 Prostitutes', 'Are Sweatshops a Necessary Evil?', 'ASBOs Infringe the Rights of Those Who are Given Them' and so on. By watching some of the clips, the issues can be discussed using other people's views and experiences and the students can be exposed to differing opinions and situations without entering the potential minefield of their own personal experiences.

TrueTube is fully moderated so students will be safe online. The clips can be downloaded so that a teacher can use them without having to rely on an internet connection. They can also be embedded into a VLE so students can watch clips again or explore topics further in their own time.

One of the more unusual and exciting features of the site as an educational resource is the ability for the students to capture and upload their own video clips. They can use the online editing facilities to create a professional-looking media clip which can be submitted to the site for moderation and possible inclusion for others to view. The use of multimedia in the classroom often stimulates interest and so motivates even disaffected learners to engage with the subject matter.

An online video drama with lesson plans and classroom resources: www.truetube.co.uk/being-victor

What can you do other than just watching a video?

1. Look at a story and present an opposing argument.
2. Write a headline for a story.
3. Analyse the argument – how does someone build their case?
4. Imagine the interview will be on TV – write an advert for it.

For pupils who have problems with speech and language:

1. First, watch silently. See if they can guess what is happening. They will be surprised how much they can understand from body language, pictures and setting.
2. Watch with sound. See if their assumptions are right.
3. Get them to note questions they have. See if others can answer them, 'Why is he angry?' or 'What time did she say she would be home?'
4. Make predictions for the next section of the show. 'What will happen next?'

Contact and information

www.truetube.co.uk

Brilliant Idea 45

A mobile phone can be the perfect safety net for vulnerable pupils

SOME SCHOOLS ARE frightened by the Bring Your Own Device (BYOD) revolution but Tupton Hall School in Chesterfield believes that mobile phones can have positive uses, especially when it comes to dealing with bullying. Bullying is very carefully monitored at Tupton Hall School. More or less equal numbers of boys and girls report incidents but the school has noticed a real gender difference. Girls tend to indulge in spiteful comments and texts and may bear grudges over long periods which can escalate out of control. Boys are much more likely to have a face-to-face confrontation.

Tupton Hall School has a whole raft of strategies in place to keep pupils safe and happy but has found that Text Someone by Contact Group has been one of the vital tools in their fight against bullying. One of the downsides of new technology is that it is easy to send unpleasant texts and even threatening phone calls. Text Someone was created to encourage young people to report incidents of bullying and anti-social behaviour directly to schools.

The students at Tupton Hall were told about the system in assembly. They were shown a PowerPoint, given a 'credit card' with key information and learnt how to report bullying, how to 'unfriend', block or report someone. They were also shown how to report abuse on Facebook, Twitter or other social media. Pupils can text information about physical bullying or might send a screen shot of abusive texts or emails. The system is available 24 hours a day, 7 days a week. This means that pupils can act straight away and not sit at home worrying about what to do. Whenever a pupil sends a message it will automatically appear on the Text Someone system in the school.

Every event is logged and investigated by the head of year who can take a view about whether the incident is a one off or is persistent, targeted and malicious. Teenagers can be very fickle and change friendship groups quite often. Most children keep mobile numbers on their phone long after a friendship has finished and can be tempted to send spiteful messages. On the other hand, children can argue but be the best of friends very soon afterwards. However, sometimes there are threats involving older siblings or relations and matters can spiral out of control.

Sue Greenwood, assistant head teacher at Tupton Hall School, believes that pupils need to know about the system long before they need it: 'Bullying is not something you can sweep under the carpet. Every school has this problem and it is important to be upfront about it and to deal with it, so we start with pupils when they are still in primary.'

There is an anti-bullying road show which starts two terms before the Year 6s arrive at their new school. Often former pupils accompany a member of the senior management team to allay worries. Next, the primary children take part in a half day workshop which features a drama production and an introduction to Text Someone. Feedback from primary schools shows that this approach is really valuable.

According to figures collated by the NSPCC:

✔ 18 per cent of children and young people who are worried about bullying said they would not talk to their parents about it.

✔ Almost half (46 per cent) of children and young people say they have been bullied at school at some point in their lives.

✔ 38 per cent of disabled children worried about being bullied.

✔ Over half (55 per cent) of lesbian, gay and bisexual young people have experienced homophobic bullying at school.

✔ 38 per cent of young people have been affected by cyber-bullying.

✔ 31,599 children called ChildLine in 2011/12 about bullying.

✔ Bullying was the main reason that boys called ChildLine.

Parents can also use the system: 'We tell them about it when they come to visit the school,' said Sue. 'Children will often say to their parents, 'Don't tell anyone about it' but parents sometimes put something in the student planner, write a note or make a phone call. Increasingly they are starting to use Text Someone.' One of the benefits is that a text is not a formal communication and so parents do not have to be too concerned about spelling and phrasing. It is also quite a spontaneous medium so parents who would postpone writing a letter are more likely to text.

Absenteeism is a common consequence of being bullied. Parents and carers often believe that the school does not deal effectively with bullying so it is important to keep them fully informed and keep records of incidents and actions taken. 'Once bullying spreads it is very hard to get rid of it from a school,' said Sue. 'It is very important to protect the most vulnerable children. Text Someone is very easy to use and everyone knows that the system works and they are very confident that action will be taken.'

Contacts and information

www.the-contactgroup.com/products/text-someone/
www.bullying.co.uk/

Brilliant Idea 46

A picture is worth so much more than a thousand words

'A SCREEN DOES suck people in,' says Ross Wallis, 'and people become addicted, but these very traits can be put to good use. My aim is that all my students should want to create, not for me, but for themselves, and computers can play a really positive role. Playing with images, creating animations, filming and gaming can be just that – playful, and fun and creative.'

Ross is Head of the Arts Faculty at Sidcot School, an independent Quaker boarding school in Somerset. He is a great enthusiast for Apple technology for art. 'The iPhone … has sparked a revolution in photography – there is even a word for it – iPhoneography. To have a small but powerful camera attached to a small but powerful computer, running a mind boggling selection of apps, all cleverly designed to enhance and distort the captured image – this power is awesome.'

Sue Stevens, a former teacher at Royal School for the Deaf in Derby and ICT trainer says, 'The ease with which we can now take and access still and moving images is what makes digital photography a very significant tool for hearing impaired children who often learn in a visual way.

'Images can give deaf and hearing impaired children the hooks upon which to hang their learning, something concrete and more accessible than the spoken word or text that needs careful reading or translation into British Sign Language (BSL). Hard to explain concepts such as solids in science can be taught more memorably through a presentation showing solids, liquids and gases. Likewise, an internet animation demonstrating the movement of blood around the body can speed up the learning process and put things into the correct context.

'Screen-based resources can be motivating and provide a more visual way to develop vocabulary in English or another language. Photographs of Warwick Castle prompted conversations about fortifications, war and how towns have defended themselves at different times. The children were able to combine their experience of a visit with an investigation of the architectural features that kept people safe. The photographs led naturally to why and because questions and also encouraged them to guess some of the answers.

'A lovely use of a digital camera is to get children to take photographs of each other and to create a Positive

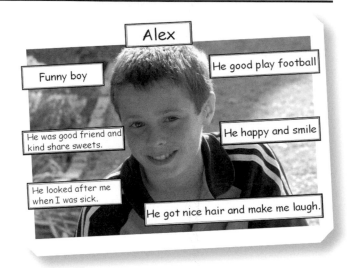

Images Wall. The addition of text boxes around each photograph allows for text to be added on screen or written on a printout and everyone has to write something nice about that person. This can be used in PSHE but also works well as a positive reinforcement for pupils with behavioural difficulties who feel nobody likes them.

'Image technology is an ideal medium for BSL users. By giving them these tools and skills we can let them tell their own stories – and more. They can be expressive and creative and will give us an insight into their view of the world.'

Ross has many suggestions for art activities, which work especially well with a smartphone or tablet:

1. Go on 'photo walks'. Students could look for circles, faces, letters of the alphabet or a colour.
2. Take a 'selfie,' cut it in half and flip it to make a symmetrical version or use this as the basis for a drawn self-portrait. The Photo Booth app will do it automatically and it provides endless hours of fun.
3. Use the camera to record a day out. Sam visited Bristol Zoo but would not draw or write. Using a camera phone, he put together a really good slide show.
4. Use pictures as an alternative to words. Jon was unhappy about writing and his sketch book stayed blank. The teachers used Comic Life app to get him to talk about photos he had taken and he created a lively and original alternative which showcased his skills. See Brilliant Idea 7.

5. Visit an art gallery and pick out favourite paintings. Find a picture of a famous artist such as Van Gogh and use the Morfo app to transform the image into a talking, 3D character who discusses the key features of his work. See Brilliant Idea 42.
6. Use the camera for stop frame animation. 'Callum had severe learning difficulties and was being bullied because of his behaviour. He decided he wanted to create a stop frame animation. He got some boys to photograph him and spent hours moving the camera incrementally until he judged it was perfect. Callum really struggled at school especially in maths. Nevertheless, he got into college to do animation, did a degree and is now working for Aardman, creators of *Wallace and Gromit*.'

You could:

✔ Use Flipshare or Shadow puppet apps to create a photo story and add an audio track or commentary. Use for school trips, interesting visitors, special days in schools or to reinforce visual timetables with photos of places and people that will be seen during the day.

✔ Investigate different lighting and aspects when taking selfies. Use to make identifying emotion support photos or visual diaries.

✔ Look at textures and patterns by going 'up close' when taking photos. Frame photos by involving something in the foreground or looking at paths and rivers to lead into the picture.

✔ Use digital images to support all areas of the curriculum, create banks of pictures for shapes around us, hidden letters, numbers or colours. Illustrate a poem or song with images or make a treasure trail.

✔ Take pictures of the school Sports Day or a visit to a museum. Use for individual work and discussion to make sure vocabulary has been assimilated and that children have grasped concepts.

✔ Make photo albums to introduce new places or experiences, such as a new school or a visit to the dentist.

✔ Use images to record processes such as bread-making.

✔ Provide visual timetables.

✔ Use with PowerPoint to create show-and-tell activities.

✔ Use Photo Story to create an automatic slide show which can be used to demonstrate a process or record achievement.

✔ Use images on interactive whiteboards, adding text and sound as necessary.

Contacts and information
www.batod.org.uk/
www.rnid.org.uk/othersites/

Photo Story: www.windowsphotostory.com/ and select download
Morfo app

Brilliant Idea 47

Mapping a child's ability

MIND MAPPING IS a very visual approach to information. Often people see it as a tool for brainstorming or for exam revision but it is also a very effective way for teachers to provide an overview of a new topic so pupils can see relationships between different parts.

At Mary Hare Grammar School they use Inspiration in many of their lessons. It is a school for profoundly deaf children in Berkshire. It is an auditory/oral school where children use written and spoken English all the time. Pupils often start the school with language delay or with a more limited vocabulary than other children of their age so staff aim to make text as accessible as possible.

'Inspiration is brilliant,' said Lesley White, Literacy Co-ordinator at Mary Hare. 'We have a site licence and all our teachers use it, in fact, it is on every computer in the school.' Teachers can create a mind map for a subject which has all the core vocabulary and key ideas in a simple visual form. Children can see the structure of what they are studying instead of having to work through text heavy material. But if the staff are good Inspiration users, the pupils are often even better. They make very creative use of mind mapping. Some are outstanding users and use it to make lots of notes in Inspiration, with illustrations from the web or clip art files to act as pegs. This helps them to structure their writing and create a text outline.

Jessica is profoundly deaf. She has only recently arrived from overseas, has minimal English but is making exceptional progress. Her class visited nearby Snelsmore Common and created mind maps. She understood the concept perfectly and produced neat detailed work, bringing in icons and images from the web to illustrate her points. Her limited vocabulary and immature syntax do not do justice to her intellectual ability but mind mapping let her show her teachers what she can do. It may take her several years to become proficient in written English but her mind map is testament to her ability to gather and manipulate information and shows that this is a girl who is very talented.

Inspiration 9 is a sophisticated thinking tool that lets users:

- Build up ideas and add images and symbols.
- Make notes, fill in gaps and develop an overview.
- Work in small groups for collaborative projects.
- Bring in multimedia files, websites.
- Develop an Outline View which can be exported into Word to create a linear essay plan.
- Find or check correct spellings.
- Extend their vocabulary with an on-the-spot dictionary/thesaurus tool.
- Export documents to a learning platform as PDFs.
- Transfer work between different devices such as a laptop, the cloud, memory stick or a tablet.

Joe Beech, a teacher with dyslexia, also recommends it. He says: 'Inspiration is a simple but very effective piece of mind mapping software which I love. It allows you to simply click and type your ideas then link them together in whatever order you like. You can then go on to link files, change icons and add notes. The beauty of this software for me is in the ability to turn the mind map into an ordered plan which you can then transfer directly into Word. I would consider using this with a class, to present work or even to plan a lesson.'

With mind mapping you could:

✔ Start with a series of questions then add answers.

✔ Write the title then add Who? What? When? Where? Why? How?

✔ Brainstorm advantages and disadvantages of having a well paid job.

✔ Categorise the principal food groups.

✔ Write a job advert then list essential and desirable qualities.

✔ Descriptive writing – think about the senses – have headings for sight, hearing, touch, taste, smell.

✔ Use it to create plans for different exam questions.

✔ Use it as a framework for a lesson plan.

Contacts and information

Inspiration: www.inspiration.com/
http://popplet.com/

The case study from Mary Hare originally appeared in *Teach Secondary* magazine (No Limits, issue 2.4, p. 64, teachsecondary.com). Reproduced by kind permission of Maze Media (2000) Ltd.

Brilliant Idea 48

Making child's play of numbers

DYSCALCULIA IS SOMETIMES known as 'number blindness' and can affect children who have no problems with other areas of the curriculum. Children with dyscalculia will have problems recognising and using number symbols, counting and understanding place value. This can affect daily life as they struggle with telling the time and estimating speed and the length of journeys. They cannot attribute numbers to temperature and find it hard to measure accurately. They may also find it difficult to work out prices and/or handle change.

One of the essential skills for children is the ability to subitise. This means being able to spot how many objects are in a group without counting. Most people can do up to ten quite accurately – think of the dots on a playing card. Children with dyscalculia find this hard. They also have problems with number bonds and so if faced with 6 + 3, they may start counting from one and lose their place.

Professor Brian Butterworth of University College London revealed that 5–7 per cent of children will have dyscalculia but that schools are not fully aware of the condition and may dismiss children as being 'not very good at maths' or label them as lazy. Professor Diana Laurillard from the London Knowledge Lab has been researching dyscalculia, focusing on computer games and apps which will help children with some of the basic skills such as number bonds, time and money. She believes that good feedback is paramount. If a computer program's response to a wrong answer is 'Try again', with no indication of why it is wrong then avoid it. Good software should model good teaching in that the child should see how to put things right.

Look for software that is engaging and motivates the pupil. A games format is good for this but avoid multiple choice as it encourages guessing rather than reasoning. Above all, make sure that the child can do something

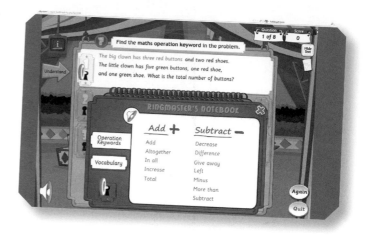

meaningful in a short time. Research shows that 20 minutes is the optimum concentration time.

Simrat Navi uses Education City. The school St Giles' Church of England Primary School in Willenhall in the West Midlands has 360 pupils. It is an inner city school with a high proportion of children on free school meals so they have been looking at ways of raising achievement using Pupil Premium funding.

Mathematics can be very abstract, especially at Key Stage 2 when they move away from using practical apparatus. Education City has brought colour and fun into the classroom. The feedback is especially important because now children don't have to ask a teacher to check their work or wait until the next day before they can see what is wrong.

Education City works well for pupils with dyscalculia, children who are not very motivated, and those with dyslexia and those on the ASD spectrum. 'It is really appealing,' said Simrat. 'It encourages independent learning and works well in our school which has workstations in many different areas.'

Contacts and information

Dynamo Maths Series: www.dynamomaths.co.uk/

Little Professor Solar – Texas Instruments: http://education.ti.com/

NumberShark: www.wordshark.co.uk/numbershark.aspx

Number Track: www.semerc.com/

Nessy Numbers: www.facebook.com/

Software from Professor Diana Laurillard's project at http://low-numeracy.ning.com/

Mental recall is an important feature of mathematics and Simrat appreciates the fact that it has captured the interest of their pupils very well. They have been working on plus and minus bonds to 20. 'It is an excellent program to encourage quick mental recall of numbers and of multiplication tables,' she said. Children work on the tables from Foundation through to Year six. The children are drawn to the eye-catching graphics and identify with the on screen figures. The pupils like the fact that they are in control; they are in the driving seat,' said Simrat. 'It is pitched at the right level and has a lively games format with different levels and rewards. They take great delight in seeing how quickly they make progress and often ask to redo exercises to see if they can get a better score.'

Brilliant Idea 49

What happens to hot ice cream?

DATALOGGING FOR CHILDREN has often been overlooked partly because teachers are not sure of how to use the equipment. Using thermometers proved fiddly and the gauge was so small that it was difficult to get an accurate or accessible reading, so for pupils with ADHD this proved to be too much as the results took such a long time to see. However, LogIT technologies came up with their LogIT Explorer datalogger which meant that pupils could easily access a range of measurements.

Danny Nicholson was teaching in a school in Southend and came across two boys who were not able to concentrate for longer than a few minutes on any task and having to share equipment proved too much for them.

'We set up an experiment based on the fact that Southend is the home of one of the most famous ice cream makers in England. Every evening after school the Rossi ice cream van was parked outside the school and sometimes he was there for a long time waiting for the children to come out of school. We decided to find out how long he would have to wait before the ice cream melted and he had to go home.'

Traditionally they would have used a thermometer to measure the temperature but using the LogITs with a temperature probe fitted meant that pupils could go and take the temperature and record on a bar chart what the temperature was every five minutes.

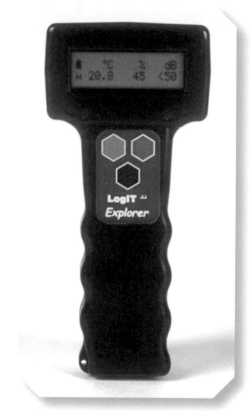

Danny started by taking the temperature of crushed ice using the LogIT and the visualiser. Everyone could see that the temperature was zero degrees. After five minutes the temperature was three degrees and the ice was melting fast.

You could:

✔ Take the temperature of the whole class to see who is the hottest/coldest.

✔ Huddle together to see if you get hotter like penguins do in the Antarctic.

✔ Use the LogITs to measure noise levels in different parts of the school.

✔ Discover which musical instrument made the loudest noise.

✔ See who can clap the loudest.

✔ Use the LogITs to measure light around the school to find where the best place to grow plants might be.

The question was then asked: 'How could the ice cream man make his ice cream last longer?'

All the children were given various materials to wrap around a plastic cup and the race was on. Bubble wrap, newspaper, cotton wool, plastic, cardboard and other materials were all used and every child had their own pot and access to a LogIT to take the temperature every two minutes. Whoever's ice was last to reach three degrees was the winner.

The two boys were engrossed in the process, the posed problem and the ease of use of the LogITs. They were keen to try the experiment again and again with different materials and charted their findings on a bar chart of time taken to thaw. They rushed out to the ice cream man the next day with their findings.

Note: Danny won't tell us which method won – you will just have to find out for yourselves!

Contact and information

LogIT Explorer: www.taglearning.com/

Brilliant Idea 50

'Come on you lazy lot, let's go adventuring!'

THE LAND OF Me brings together all the best elements of a classic picture story book and ICT. There are six chapters, each with a different theme, which follow the exploits of Buddy Boo the bear, Eric the raccoon and Willow the owl. The adventure unfolds on screen but what happens there is only a small part of the story. Children can make music, construct buildings, choreograph dances and create monsters and more. There are over 100 printable activities, games and puzzles to do away from the computer.

The company Made in Me has worked with Professor John Siraj-Blatchford at Swansea University's Centre for Child Research to make sure that every activity is founded on the most effective techniques for developing language and creativity in young children. Chapter one focuses on shape, size and colour but these themes spawn lots of adjectives too – big, round, purple – so teachers can develop and record receptive language to see how much children understand or use the story as the basis for work on descriptions in literacy. The Land of Me has been used in Early Years settings, primary and in different ways in some special schools and home-based learning. The teaching activities are also geared to support a cross-curricular approach to incorporate science, geography and history as well as creative activities such as art and dance.

Cuckmere House School is a community special school in Seaford, East Sussex for boys aged between five years to sixteen years old who need help with behavioural, emotional and social difficulties. Staff used Chapter two, 'The World Outside', to develop games and activities to support personal, social and emotional well-being. Pupils had to choose from a selection of clothing and materials as to the most appropriate for differing weather conditions and environments. They identified each item as it was pulled out of a bag and matched it with the weather and/or terrain it would be used in.

Once all the items were laid out on the floor the teacher would create a 'desert', 'lake' or 'arctic' setting, as in The Land of Me, and the children would then choose an appropriate piece of clothing. Some were not able to do this. As well as looking at weather and climate, they looked at day and night and time zones as these are very relevant to the adventures. Staff found that several pupils needed help with telling the time and using the 24-hour clock.

After working through the story and the related activities, the school realised they needed to refine their personal learning programmes with a greater emphasis on life skills. The Land of Me provided a stimulus and framework for a host of activities as well as being lots of fun.

You could:

✔ Go onto The Land of Me blog (www.madeinme.com/blog/category/free-activities/) and try out the free activities which include matching games and making story dice.

✔ Read the case studies on the site which show how it can be used for music, art and craft activities.

Contacts and information

The work from Cuckmere House School will form part of a new pack of teachers' materials for The Land of Me.
www.madeinme.com/the-land-of-me/

Part 2

Now it's your turn

Brilliant Starter 1

Using Popplet or Padlet

Collaboration or Mind mapping on an iPad

➲ Download the app called Popplet Lite (free) from the app store.

➲ From the four icons under the words 'my popplet' choose the colour blocks to choose the background colour for your mind map.

➲ Choose the cog wheel to 'make new popple'.

➲ The rectangle that appears has four icons along the bottom. The first changes the colour of the frame, the second (T) brings up an additional toolbar to choose the alignment and size of your text. The last two allow you to draw in the rectangle or insert or take a photo.

➲ Touch and drag the rectangle to reposition or touch and drag the triangles on the corners to resize.

➲ Lastly, touch the small circles outside the rectangle to add another, connected popple. Touch and drag to a suitable position.

➲ To return to a popple to edit it, just touch the rectangle to select it and all the editing tools will reappear.

➲ To enlarge the completed popple or reduce it in size, simply pinch with two fingers (or select the view all option in the top left corner of the screen) or expand with two fingers to enlarge or zoom in.

➲ The clear all button will erase all your popples. The cross in the top right of the individual popple erases a single popple. If there is no longer a connecting line between popples, drag a circle from one popple to another to connect them.

➲ A popplet mind map, once completed, can be exported or saved as an image (jpeg) or emailed as a pdf.

Padlet is a word wall to enable a group of people to collaborate on their learning

➲ Go to padlet.com and open a wall.

➲ Double click anywhere on the wall to add a text box, a link, a file or an image.

➲ To share this with others go to the cog wheel and choose the address tab.

➲ From here you can copy the address of the wall to display and share or create your own address.

➲ All students can then double click from their machines to add comments or findings.

➲ The end result can be exported in a number of different file formats.

Brilliant Starter 2

Using the Book Creator app or Publisher to make a book

When you open the Book Creator, look at the short tutorial or follow these basic instructions:

⮕ Click on new book at the top left of the screen.

⮕ Choose the size and orientation of your book. Landscape is lovely for picture books or photo collections and portrait or square books lend themselves to text plus images.

⮕ At the top right there are three icons.

   ⮕ The **plus** sign enables you to choose to insert photos, immediate camera shots, drawings, text or put in a sound.

   ⮕ **The sound** can be recorded immediately when the red button is clicked and will go straight into your page or you can choose music or audio that is stored in your iTunes library.

   ⮕ If you go to the **i** button (with the sound tab highlighted) there is a choice to make your recorded hotspot invisible. This means you could place it over your images or drawings to encourage readers to investigate the page! Click on the Page tab if you wish the sound or music to carry on throughout the whole book, even when the pages are turned, by enabling the sound track.

⮕ The other function of the i button is to change the background page colour and set grid guides if you wish to position items accurately.

⮕ Adding text is straightforward but you can click the mic icon on the keyboard (to the left of the spacebar) to record your words and it will then type it straight into your book.

⮕ The rectangle icon with the arrow pointing upwards enables you to share your work. iBooks will support any sounds you have entered in your book.

⮕ On the top left hand side of your screen are three more icons.

⮕ Undo will undo the selected action.

⮕ Pages allow you to review and reorder the pages by clicking the edit option, waiting for the pages to wobble then press and hold to re-sequence your book.

➲ My books takes you back to all the books you have created. In this view, click the + option to combine books allowing for collaborative work to be combined into a single book or even duplicate your book. The i options allows you to rename or retitle or delete the book.

Using Publisher to make a printable book:

➲ Click on Publications to Print.

➲ Choose Catalog (American spelling!). Select your favourite design.

➲ Use the Objects toolbar to replace the picture… click on the picture icon, draw a frame.

➲ Around the area to put the picture in, select either ClipArt or Picture from file and choose a picture. Resize as appropriate.

➲ In the panel on the left hand side you can choose different colour or font styles.

➲ In that same panel you can choose the design or different picture for each page.

➲ This will make a folded book… it's important to work out the page order!

Brilliant Starter 3

Using Audio Notetaker

This is a wonderful audio recorder that has many original functions. It is possible to edit the audio very simply but the ability to segment and colour code different aspects of speech is so effective.

⮕ Open Audio Notetaker and click on the File icon, top left hand side of the screen.

⮕ Choose New.

⮕ To import an audio file, click on the import icon (a square with an arrow pointing down).

⮕ The audio file will insert itself in chunks which make it easy to listen to and colour according to speakers, arguments, facts or figures of speech.

⮕ To colour the blocks of text, click on the block and click on the colours to colour code your work. There are different templates that have ready-made codes. Go to the right hand pane to locate the drop down arrow.

⮕ To delete or edit a block, click on the block and press the delete key on the keyboard. Split individual chunks by clicking on it and choosing split chunk from the right hand pane.

⮕ To insert your own audio by recording, click on the red spot on the top left hand corner of the screen. As you speak, the audio blocks will appear in the main window.

⮕ Once again, you can colour and organise the blocks.

⮕ To move chunks of audio, highlight the block and drag it to the new location.

⮕ It is possible to add text to annotate or support the audio file. Just click in the left hand panel and type.

⮕ To add images to the audio file go to the import button and import images. The image will pop straight into another pane to the left of the text pane. Sometimes the image does not appear fully and if you click on the truncate icon just above the pane it will reveal the whole image.

⮕ Exporting the resulting file can be done in a variety of ways; as audio, album and video. It is possible to present the finished annotated and illustrated audio file as a presentation similar to PowerPoint. Click on the screen image icon to reveal your presentation.

Brilliant Starter 4

Using digital images

Using your camera, phone, ipad or tablet

Your camera:

○ It should have a download lead that plugs into the camera via a small plug and then into your computer or laptop via a normal USB. It may also have a SD card that slots into a port on the side of your computer.

○ The camera needs to be switched to download on the dial or sliding switch that selects whether you will be using still images or video. This symbol usually looks like a rectangle with an arrow pointing away from it (but this can vary from camera to camera).

○ As soon as the camera is connected in this way, and is switched on, a window will appear asking you what you would like to do with the pictures. You may want to find the images via the My Computer or Documents section of your computer where you will find the camera or SD card recognised as another drive.

○ Select what you want to do with the pictures!

○ Do remember which folder you have downloaded your pictures to... many the time that I have spent trying to discover where I have downloaded my pictures!

○ Another possibility is to take and store your photos in 'the Cloud'. Dropbox, google Drive or iCloud are all places to store photos so that they are accessible to you from any machine.

○ Flikr and many other photo sharing websites store photos so that anyone can view them. With all of these facilities it is essential that you ensure your photos are only shared with those people you want to see them. Experiment first to ensure security and safety especially if the facility allows public searching.

iPads, iPhones, tablets and android phones:

○ All these have apps that allow photos to be shared locally such as Airdrop, Skydrive or Bump.

○ There is also the possibility of sharing with Facebook but, as Facebook changes security settings frequently, privacy cannot be ensured.

○ PicLab is a free photo editing app for Apple and Android that can manipulate images or Sktchy (iPad) which will allow you to make portraits from your photos, but there are many, many more.

Computer:

○ Websites such as www.bighugelabs.com allow you to make posters, stamps, magazine covers and photo albums with your photos.

○ Photostory 3 will allow you to download photos to make presentations.

○ Your photos can now be used in your interactive whiteboard software, wordprocessing software or downloaded onto digital photoframes to scroll through selections of photos automatically.

Brilliant Starter 5

Using sound and easy-speak microphones

There is an excellent, simple to use, free software download which is incorporated in the easy-speak mic (http://audacity.sourceforge.net/) which can be used to record sounds and then edit them and add effects.

If using the easy-speak mic:

➲ Switch on the on/off switch at the side of the microphone to 'on'.

➲ Press and release the red, record button. The LED will go red meaning you are recording (if it doesn't, press it again!).

➲ Press and release the red, record button to stop recording.

➲ Press the green button to play your recording.

➲ To play different tracks, press play (green button) then forward or back on the yellow buttons (just above the on/off switch).

➲ The middle yellow button (*) toggles between MP3 recordings and WAV files.

To download a file:

➲ Insert the USB into your computer (pull off the end of the microphone).

➲ Navigate to the files ... go to Removable disk/mic rec file and find your file from there.

➲ This is the easiest way to delete files (right mouse click on the file and choose delete).

To download into Audacity:

➲ Open Audacity… go to File/open and navigate to the file.

➲ Select and edit as shown below.

If using your computer's inbuilt mic or another plug in mic:

➲ Connect your microphone and use record, stop and play buttons to hear your work.

➲ The audio track appears as you record.

➲ If you record further then a second audio track appears underneath. Both tracks are then played at once. The double ended arrow icon will allow you to move tracks along to accommodate different sounds.

➲ Clicking mute prevents a track being played. Clicking solo ensures only the selected track is played.

➲ Once audio tracks are recorded you can use the select tool (I bar) to drag over a piece and use the edit menu to cut or copy sounds. They can be combined onto one track or different tracks can be used for different types of sounds.

➲ To hear part of a track select it and then click play.

➲ Click on edit and then silence to insert a silence.

➲ Edit/split takes the highlighted section out and moves it onto a new track leaving a rest in its place.

➲ To use effects, highlight your piece of sound and then click on effects and select from the drop down options. Effects work cumulatively, one on top of the other until you turn them off. You can use undo as many times as you need to when using effects.

Brilliant Starter 6

Using Inspiration, the mind mapping tool for notes and links

The Create Tool allows you to add a new linked cell in the direction you choose. Moving the cursor over the Create button will highlight the direction for a new cell.

- ➲ Select the required symbol.

- ➲ Click over direction point on Create button.

- ➲ Type in the details.

- ➲ Press Shift-Enter.

Using the RapidFire tool

- ➲ Select the required symbol.

- ➲ Click on the RapidFire button.

- ➲ Type details and then press Enter.

- ➲ Point and Type.

- ➲ Click anywhere in an open area.

- ➲ Type information required then click away from symbol.

Using the Symbol palette

- ➲ You can replace a symbol with one from the Symbol palette.

- ➲ Select the required symbol.

- ➲ On Symbol palette, click Select Library button and choose category and select.

Drag and Drop

➲ You can add a symbol from the Symbol palette using drag and drop.

➲ On Symbol palette, click Select Library button and choose category.

➲ Drag the symbol to position it and then release the mouse button.

Using the Link Tool

➲ Select symbol for start of link and then click on the Link button.

➲ Click the symbol for the end of the link.

➲ Add text on the link and click on the required link.

➲ Then type in the text details and click anywhere to deselect.

Adding Notes

➲ Select the required symbol.

➲ Click on the Note button.

➲ Then type in the details of the Note.

Transfer to Word

➲ Save Inspiration document as normal and click on the Transfer button to create a word document.

Exporting diagrams

➲ Click File, Export and select Format & Option.

➲ Click Save then select Folder and type File name.

Brilliant Starter 7

Creating your first blog post

Select your blogging provider. Some tailor made sites for schools are Kidblog, Edublog or Primary Blogger.

➲ Sign up and select the privacy settings. This is really important and will establish who can see posts, who can comment on posts and who will write posts. Take some time to consider this carefully. Sometimes it is better to set very strict privacy at first until students get used to the idea of blogging.

➲ Add users to your class. It is important that you allocate each entry a status such as student, adult, teacher or administrator. This will mean that you can assign permissions to groups of people on your blog.

➲ This should be the time to discuss safety issues with your bloggers. It is so important to impress upon them the 'do's' and 'don'ts' of blogging.

➲ Don't mention names, addresses or personal details.

➲ Don't divulge your password.

➲ Do be pleasant, constructive and positive in your writing.

➲ Do comment on posts but always be as polite as you would be in the 'real' world.

➲ Enjoy writing for lots of different people. They will be really interested in your posts if they are written carefully and are interesting.

➲ Now go to New Post and type in your first entry. There will be a title box followed by a text box designed to house your blog post. Formatting should be available above the text box and an icon to upload any media from your computer. You will need to select and upload any media first and then use the image in your blog post.

➲ It is always a good idea to preview your post and edit it before publishing it.

➲ Decide whether you would prefer to restrict the ability to comment on the post. This might be advisable at first.

➲ Check and select if you want your blog to be publicly visible or private. Once again it might be a good idea to restrict this to private initially.

➲ Decide if it is necessary to save the draft to work on it later. Associate some tag words to the blog to enable effective searching later on and then…

➲ Publish!

Brilliant Starter 8

Creating links and animation in Office and IWB software

⊃ Creating links in IWB software or Word documents enables you to jump straight to a relevant page or website without having to search.

⊃ This is particularly useful when linking in planning documents or in IWB software.

⊃ To create a link to a website, sound file or another page usually you make a right click after you have highlighted the word or image.

⊃ This will take you to a drop down menu that will list the activities that you can associate with the highlighted property.

⊃ In PowerPoint this list will display a 'hyperlink' option which enables you to choose a website, file or page in your presentation to link to.

⊃ In the ribbon at the top, after you have selected the 'insert' tab, there are also quick links to insert a video or audio file (look at the right hand end of the insert ribbon)

⊃ In PowerPoint these options only appear in 'design' mode. In Smart Notebook or ActivInspire a simple right click will display the options.

⊃ In all programs it is wise to link the whole image rather than rely on a tiny link icon appearing in the corner but with text it will turn blue with an underline under the chosen text.

Inserting custom animation into PowerPoint or object animation/ page animation in IWB software

By putting in custom animation, PowerPoint is transformed into a fun format for pupils to write and enjoy their own stories.

Putting in custom animation:

⊃ Insert a picture or text.

⊃ Click on it so that small circular placeholders appear.

⊃ Go to the animation tab and all sorts of animations will appear.

⊃ Click on the downwards arrow for even more options and scroll down to the bottom of this window to reveal Custom Animation. This enables you to draw your own path!

⊃ Animation in Smart Notebook

➲ Go to the properties tab at the side of Notebook to find page recording which will animate everything you do on the page and replay it.

➲ Select an object to animate and object animation appears in the properties toolbar and options appear for that particular object.

Brilliant Starter 9

Using iMovie on the iPad

⮑ Open up the app and choose theater (American spelling!).

⮑ Tap the + sign and choose Movie… from this page, choose Create Movie.

⮑ From the three-pane window choose videos or photos in the top right… when you press your chosen video go to the curving downwards arrow to insert it into the timeline in the bottom pane.

⮑ You may want to select a project theme by clicking on the cog wheel in the bottom right hand corner. From here it is possible to choose a theme, music and fade in and out facilities.

⮑ Tap the video to enable the bottom toolbar to appear. This toolbar will enable you to split the video and delete parts of it. Move the video along past the timeline to where you want to split or crop the video. Press Split in the bottom right hand toolbar. Move the video along a bit more. Press Split again to isolate a chunk of video and then select that bit of video to delete by selecting it then pressing the dustbin icon.

⮑ Select a still image to put at the beginning of your video, select it and press Title. Options for the kind of animation you would like to have for your title can be found by pressing the T on the toolbar. Click on the words to edit to the title of your choice, then press Done on the toolbar.

⮑ The microphone icon will enable you to record your own commentary or you can choose Audio on the top toolbar to select some music from your iTunes library. There are themes and sound effects here as well.

⮑ Flick the video through to the end to attach another still image on which to put your Title/closing credits.

⮑ If there is more than one bit of video, there may be some transitions in between them. By clicking on the bowtie it is possible to change the style of transition.

⮑ If all these descriptions are just too much, by clicking on the question mark at the top left of the screen, labels appear next to all the icons.

⮑ To finish, press the back arrow at the top left of the screen and this view will show you a thumbnail of your video with the title, length and date of your movie and under that are the play, share and delete icons.

⮑ You have made your first iMovie!

Adapting Word

Choosing the best font

⮕ The fonts you choose are really important. Choose an illegible curly font and the task of reading the text becomes much harder even though it might look prettier! The default is Times New Roman but you can set your own default.

⮕ Look for the grey word 'Font' beneath the font options on the Home tab.

⮕ Look for the tiny arrow pointing to the bottom right hand corner of the screen.

⮕ This will open the font setting window from where you can choose the font style, size and colour and click on 'set as default' for the computer to automatically select this format when it opens.

Using tables

⮕ Click on the tables icon in the Insert tab.

⮕ Click on the first cell and extend your mouse diagonally to the right until you have included as many rows and columns as you need.

⮕ To insert a picture or text, just click inside the cell and insert the picture.

⮕ To alter the first column whilst leaving the other columns of equal width, hold down Ctrl whilst moving the cell line.

⮕ The tables ribbon that automatically opens when drawing a table will allow you to colour, merge and filter your table. There are design and format options tabs to use to refine your work.

Using shapes

⮕ The shapes can be accessed via the Insert tab. There are lots of certificates, speech bubbles as well as a host of fun shapes to use in posters.

⮕ Next to them are the SmartArt options to add design elements to your handouts or worksheets.

⮕ To write inside any of the shapes, right mouse click and select Add text.

⮕ The shapes ribbon will automatically open up to reveal more options.

Using bullets and borders

⮕ Bullets, especially if they are picture bullets, are a great way of breaking up big blocks of text.

⮕ Click on the bullet icon in the Home tab, click on the drop down menu and choose Define new bullet.

⮕ Click on symbol, picture or font for a range of options.

⮕ Click on symbol and choose Webdings or Wingdings from the drop down menu and a whole range of pictures and symbols should appear. Choose one and click on OK.

Borders

⮫ Borders just make documents look more appealing!

⮫ Click on the Page Borders tab and choose Page Borders or Page color (American spelling!) and then look for the Art drop down menu at the bottom of the window. There are lots of great borders to choose from.

Importing and watermarking images

⮫ Importing images is very straightforward. Click on the Insert tab and then navigate to your own picture (or choose Clip art and type in the subject for a choice of clip art images).

⮫ When the image goes into your document a ribbon appears called Picture Tools, Format which allows you to format the image and 'wrap' text around the picture i.e. move it about or watermark the image into the back of your document so that you can type over it, right click and select 'wrap text'.

⮫ There are numerous options here to change the saturation of the image or remove the background.

Brilliant Starter 11

Choosing a suitable spelling program

There are lots of programs on the market to help with phonics, letter blends and to help children develop an eye and an ear for spelling. Here are some guidelines to help you choose the ones which will be effective with your learners.

Is the display clear?

➲ For learners who have problems with information processing, a cluttered screen with distracting colours and movement can hinder understanding.

Does it feature anagrams?

➲ For learners with dyslexia, this is not a good idea!

Can the speed of presentation and response be altered?

➲ A program that flashes information onto the screen too quickly or requires a reaction beyond the capabilities of the learner will encourage guessing instead of a considered response; a program that moves too slowly will result in poor concentration. A long introduction is useful first time round, but becomes boring once you know it too well.

Can the length of the game be altered?

➲ A good game will allow the teacher to decide the number of goes or the success rate to be achieved for successful completion.

Can the sound level be altered?

➲ A nasty noise that broadcasts the fact that you have made an error is not helpful for some learners.

Does the program save the settings?

➲ It is a boon in a busy schedule if next time you come to the program, you can continue with the same options.

Does the program encourage the learner to work independently?

➲ Is the task clear? Will the learner need to read on-screen instructions in order to tackle the required task? Are essential instructions spoken and/or can they be read by a screen reader if needed?

The teacher chose a program for Hugh, with target words within his reading level. The 'carrier language' which is the on-screen instructions and sentences surrounding the target words were too advanced, leaving Hugh unable to work independently.

Can word lists be edited?

➲ A good program will allow the teacher to enter word lists designed to support the learner's learning and to include subject-specific vocabulary.

What happens when the learner makes a mistake?

➲ There is nothing worse than getting caught in a loop where the software will not continue unless you get the answer right but provides no help if you get it wrong.

Does it use rewards and penalties?

➲ James, Year 6, loved playing a spelling game where if he got the word wrong, a little man would appear on the screen, pick up the word, screw it up and throw it into a dustbin. Unfortunately, James found it more fun to get the word wrong! Here the penalties were more attractive than the rewards and got in the way of learning.

Are there home user versions of the program?

➲ Parents often appreciate being involved and if there is a home version of the program it can provide a focus for targeted work. These programs provide structure and often have a fun, competitive element, which is a boon when it comes to homework.

Brilliant Starter 12

Using Clicker 6

It is so easy to use Clicker 6 now. The options are straightforward but there are some functions that make it easy for you to set up for your class and reduce the amount of support needed.

Making Clicker sets

➲ Open a document or book template.

➲ Locate the Clicker set option on the top left hand side of the screen.

➲ From the options choose the quick grid wizard and choose the word bank.

➲ When the window opens you can type in a set of words or copy and paste a text.

➲ Look carefully at the right hand side of the window. This is where you can set the level at which the person is working. You can filter out some high frequency words or words with fewer letters in.

➲ Underneath these choices are a way of selecting the style of word bank.

➲ Alphabetical will mean that all the words are stored under different letter tab, one grid stores them all on one grid up to 32 words.

➲ Create will apply all these choices and deliver a grid that should support the work that you are doing.

Writing with Clicker 6

➲ Clicker 6 has all the same functions as before. A right click speaks the word in the grid, a left click sends the word to the document and a shift and left click will allow editing.

➲ On the top toolbar or at the bottom right hand side of the screen there is a small grid next to the cog wheel icon. This small grid activates the predictor. As you type or select words to go to the document, a selection of words appear for pupils to choose from. These words can speed the writing process by predicting what is most likely to follow the selected word. A right click on top of the word will also read the word to check if it is suitable.

➲ All text can be read back and portions of the text will be read as soon as a full stop is inserted.

➲ Now you can get started. There are so many different types of books, writing frames and activities you can write with Clicker 6 and the Cricksoft website has video tutorials to support the software.

Brilliant Starter 13

Using GarageBand

- Open GarageBand and make sure New Project and piano are selected or the podcast icon if you wish to record your voice.

- Click on choose and select a destination and title for your track and click Create.

- In the window that opens, choose a category of sound file from the right hand window and a selection of clips will appear under the category panel.

- Drag a clip onto your editing window (in the middle of the screen and drop it in the correct position).

- Try dragging another sound file onto the track and you will find it drops in underneath the previous one.

- To move the tracks just click and drag.

- To make one track fade in or out or just become quieter click on the small drop down arrow on the left hand side of the track (it is in a small toolbar).

- An editing track appears and if you click underneath your track on the line a dot will appear. Click again a bit further along and you will be able to drag the line up or down to alter the volume.

- To listen to your track click on the space bar on your keyboard to start or stop the track playing.

- The return key on your keyboard returns the playhead line to the beginning of your composition.

- To save your song, click on Share from the toolbar at the top of your screen, click on export and choose a destination.

- Click on save to complete your first composition using GarageBand.

Brilliant Starter 14

Using I Can Animate

- ⮑ Connect a camera to your computer.

- ⮑ Click on Camera to start capturing your movie.

- ⮑ To capture a frame, click on the Capture button. You can also use the keyboard shortcut Control-Enter or the number 1.

- ⮑ Use the numbers 2 to 9 to capture that number of frames if you want the action to pause for a small time, 3 is usually a good choice and gives a smoother result.

- ⮑ Note: Click in the Frames View or in the Preview Area before using the numbers 1 to 9 to capture a frame or frames.

- ⮑ When you have captured a frame, a small thumbnail will appear in the Frames View at the bottom of the main window.

- ⮑ Make some small appropriate changes to the items you are animating and capture another frame.

- ⮑ Continue to do this until you have finished the action you wish to create. You should also regularly save your work.

- ⮑ To save your work, choose File > Save from the menu bar. A dialogue will open asking you to choose a location and a file name for your project.

- ⮑ Click on the Play button to play back your sequence of frames.

- ⮑ Choose File > Export from the menu bar.

and I Can Present

- Set up a green screen against a wall with even light falling onto it.

- Connect a camera to your computer if your computer doesn't have an inbuilt camera.

- Connect a microphone if your computer doesn't have an inbuilt microphone.

- Open the software and click on backgrounds.

- From this menu choose a suitable photo background. If there are no suitable ones in the categories listed, click on import and browse for your own photo or image saved onto your computer.

- When you have found a suitable photo click on choose.

- Then type in any text you wish to appear on the autocue in the text box below the picture.

- Click on Recording studio.

- You may need to select the camera you have connected by clicking on the Video input drop down menu.

- You may need to choose a microphone from the audio input drop down menu.

- Now the magic happens! All the green background will have become transparent and your picture will appear behind the person sitting in front of the camera.

- When you click on the red camera button you will get a five second countdown and the recording will start.

- Click on the grey camera button to finish.

- Your video will immediately playback the recording.

- Click on Export to export your video and choose a suitable format and destination. Your video will then be ready to play independently from the program.

Brilliant Starter 15

Creating an app with AppFurnace

⮕ Click on the Create App button and type a title in the input box.

⮕ You should be able to see three panels in the layout tool:

  ⮕ On the left are a collection of user interface widgets that you can use to build your app.

  ⮕ On the right are controls to change the properties of the currently selected page or widget.

  ⮕ Finally, in the middle column you will see a representation of the iPhone screen.

Pages and widgets

⮕ A **page** is a full screen 'canvas' upon which you can place widgets – user interface components such as text labels and images.

⮕ You can add buttons to enable the user to navigate between pages.

⮕ To change the page's name, or its background colour, use the property controls in the right column.

⮕ Click on the box tab and use the colour picker to change the colour of the page.

⮕ **Widgets** are user interface components that you can add to pages to display a piece of text, or an image, a video, a twitter feed and so on. These can be found in the left hand panel.

Adding a label

⮕ Click on Label on the left panel.

⮕ The white area on the right of this panel shows the various label styles that are already in the system.

⮕ To add a label to the page, click on the top widget (for example where it says 'Text') to select it, and then drag and drop it onto the page canvas in the middle of the screen.

Set the label properties

⮕ Click on the word Text and a yellow box should appear around it.

⮕ You could drag it around the page now or resize it using the grabber in the bottom right corner.

⮕ Click on the settings ('cog') icon and type 'Test' in the text input box.

⮕ Click on Save to save your work.

Preview your app

⮩ Click on the Preview button at the top of the screen.

⮩ You should see a white screen with the words 'Test'.

Tweaking the widget's appearance

⮩ Click on the Test label again to change the fields in the text and shape tabs.

Adding pages

⮩ At the bottom of the left panel click on Add, and a second page should appear.

⮩ Click on the button widget and drag it onto the page.

Making the buttons change the page

⮩ Go to Page 1 and select the button there.

⮩ Go to the settings tab in the property grid and use the drop down next to the word 'navigate' in the 'tapped' section to select Page 2.

⮩ Select the page by clicking an empty part of the background (or the Page 1 button under the Pages heading) and set the animation drop down to 'Slide Right' to control how the page appears on screen.

Preview your app

⮩ Click on the Preview button at the top of the screen to see your app in action.

Using iMovie

⮕ Connect the digital video camcorder to the computer with the firewire cord.

⮕ Turn on camcorder.

⮕ Select iMovie program.

⮕ Double click on the iMovie folder, then the iMovie icon.

⮕ Make sure your machine is set on Thousands of Colours on the control strip.

⮕ Click on New Project.

⮕ Title your movie and click on Create.

Recording live

⮕ Press PLAY on the camcorder and your video should be displayed on the LCD display screen on the camcorder and the computer.

Importing digital video into a movie

⮕ Make sure the Mode Switch is set to Camera mode or use the Camera playback controls to view the tape in the iMovie screen on the computer.

⮕ Click the PLAY button.

⮕ When the iMovie monitor displays the scene you want to use, click the Import button to begin importing.

⮕ To stop importing, click the Import button again.

⮕ Select a clip, drag it down to the Timeline at the bottom and use play controls underneath to review clip.

Splitting video clips

⮕ Click on the clip to select it.

⮕ Move the playhead (red line) to where you want to split it.

⮕ Choose Split Video Clip at Playhead from the Edit menu.

⮕ If you want to remove part of the clip, click on it to select it, and click on delete.

Adding and editing titles

⮕ Select a title style from the list in the middle of the Titles panel.

⮕ To speed up or slow down the titling effect, adjust the speed and/or pause sliders.

➲ If a title scrolls, you can change the direction it scrolls by clicking on the arrows on the direction button.

➲ Drag the title from the list in the middle of the Titles panel to the clip viewer.

➲ If you want the title to appear over a clip, place it before that clip. A title icon appears between the clips, and a small progress bar appears under it.

Adding scene transitions

➲ Transitions smooth the cuts between scenes (clips).

➲ Click the Transitions button (T).

➲ Select a transition in the Transitions panel.

➲ Drag the transition from the Transitions panel to the desired location in the timeline viewer.

Adding music: to record audio CD music into your movie

➲ Click the Audio button.

➲ Insert the audio CD into your computer's CD-ROM drive.

➲ If the CD automatically starts playing through your computer's speaker, stop it by clicking the Play button on the Audio panel.

➲ Select a track in the Audio panel and do one of the following:

➲ Drag the audio CD track from the panel to audio track 1 or 2 in the timeline viewer.

➲ Click the Record Music button on the Audio panel to start recording music into your movie. To end recording, click the Stop button.

Extracting audio from a video clip

➲ If a video clip already contains audio when you import it, you can remove it from the clip. In the timeline viewer, select the video clip that contains the audio you want to extract.

➲ Choose Extract Audio from Advanced on the menu bar. The extracted audio appears in audio track 1.

➲ When you extract audio, you copy (not remove) it from the video clip.

➲ However, iMovie turns the volume of the video clip all the way down when you extract the audio, so you won't hear the audio in the original video clip anymore.

➲ When you have finished creating your iMovie, go to File > Export Movie > Export.

➲ You can then choose how to export the file and where to save it.

Brilliant Starter 17

Using Movie Maker

➲ Connect a video camera to your computer and open the software.

➲ In the Movie Tasks pane, under Capture Video, click Capture from video device.

➲ On the Video Capture Device page, in Available devices, click your camera, then Next.

➲ Enter a file name for your captured video and choose Best quality for playback on my computer as a setting.

➲ Click Next.

➲ Click Start Capture and press play on your camera. Movie Maker will begin transferring video to your computer.

➲ Your clips will be in the Collection pane. Double click on a clip to play it in the preview window. Drag the clips you want to use onto the storyboard at the bottom of the screen.

➲ To rearrange your clips on the storyboard, just drag and drop them to a different location.

You can edit your clips to make sure you keep only the footage you want.

➲ Switch from storyboard to timeline view (click Show Timeline, just above the storyboard).

➲ Click the clip you want to edit; you will see small black arrows at each end of the clip, and a blue timeline marker.

➲ If you want to cut footage from the beginning of the clip, click on the left hand arrow and drag it slowly to the right until you reach the point you want – you will be able to see where you are in the preview window.

Audio tracks can be added to your movie

➲ First, in Capture Video in the Tasks menu, click Import audio or music. Browse your way to where your audio/music is stored, and select the files you want to use. They will appear as part of your collection.

➲ Drop in the clip and trim to fit as before.

➲ Right-clicking on the Audio/Music track will give a menu which allows you to modify your added audio. Fade In and Fade Out are particularly useful (they help to make transitions smoother). You can do the same with the audio track which is attached to your video clip – it's sometimes useful to mute this if you don't need the soundtrack you have recorded.

You can change the way one clip leads into the next by adding video transitions.

➲ In the Movie Tasks pane, under Edit Movie, click View video transitions. Select the transition effect you would like, and drag it to the transition cell between the two clips you are working on.

Finally, you can add titles, captions and credits to your film:

➲ In the Movie Tasks pane, under Edit Movie, click Make titles or credits. This gives you the option of creating a title as an opening sequence to your film, credits to go at the end, or captions before/on/after any clip. Simply type text in the box, choose your font, background colour and title animation,

➲ Click 'Done, add title to movie' when you have finished.

Brilliant Starter 18

Using Photostory3

- ⤵ Download Photostory3 from the Microsoft website.

- ⤵ Select begin a new story. Other options are to edit or play a story.

- ⤵ Click on import pictures to browse for images you want to use.

- ⤵ The imported pictures appear on a track underneath and can be re-ordered by clicking on the picture and then arrows.

- ⤵ Clicking on effect below a picture that is being displayed enables you to select from a range of picture effects.

- ⤵ Click Next. Click on each picture in turn and add labels by typing into the text box. Text options are available above this to change font and position text.

- ⤵ Use the red record button to record your narration to the images.

- ⤵ Use the preview button to watch your photo story.

- ⤵ Click Next.

- ⤵ Use the customise motion button to set the transition between pictures and the start and end points of any motion by dragging the handles.

- ⤵ Add background music by clicking on select music to browse for any music on your computer.

- ⤵ The create music button allows you to select from options to create your own music.

- ⤵ Save your story allows you to select from a number of save options depending on what you want to use the photo story for. Make sure you also save your work as a project as you may want to edit and reuse it later.

- ⤵ Click on Next, browse to a place to save your movie file and save. This will take a few moments to save all aspects of your movie.

Brilliant Starter 19

Creating a comic with Comic Life

⮕ Select a template for your new page or you can create your own layout by dragging panels anywhere you want them.

⮕ Add digital images from your library, other disks or a connected digital camera. You can drag and drop images into the Comic Life interface (from your library or any connected disk), or you can drag items directly from the camera's DCIM file into Comic Life.

⮕ Dragging an image onto a panel will put the image into the panel and crop it so the shortest dimension of the image matches the shortest dimension of the panel. You can adjust the panel size/shape separately from the image's size.

⮕ Select a style/filter for digital images. You can leave your images in their unfiltered state, but Comic Life's built-in filters and styles give you some very cool control over how 'comicy' your comic looks. If you don't like the predefined styles, you can enter your own filter settings to get that perfect look.

⮕ Don't overlook the fact that you can draw your own images (on the computer, or on paper and scan them in) and then include them in your comic once they are in a digital format.

⮕ Add text containers and text. Just like almost everything else in Comic Life, adding text is a simple drag and drop process. The text containers at the bottom of the window provide you with different text presentations.

⮕ Drag a container into your page and enter your text. If you have a balloon selected, you can drag the tail to associate the speech or thought with a particular character in an image.

⮕ Additional tails can be added for more than one speaker at a time.

⮕ Other text containers have options for styles and effects to enhance the text. The controls allow you to stretch, scale, skew, colorize, outline, shade and too many other options to list.

⮕ The predefined options are numerous and individual controls let you take them further.

⮕ Save (frequently) and export to your format of choice. The HTML export creates an interface that allows users to 'flip' through your comic page-by-page.

⮕ Big Huge Labs, www.bighugelabs.com, has a free Captioner that enables you to quickly make a comic-style poster from your own digital images. These have 'wows' and 'pows' to add as well. This free program is great for posters, labels and jokes.

Brilliant Starter 20

A quick start to using Excel

This starter will take you through the basic skills needed to make a spreadsheet. The terms needed to understand these instructions are:

➲ Cells: individual boxes on the screen.

➲ Columns: delineated by letters, the columns go vertically down the screen.

➲ Rows: delineated by numbers, rows go horizontally across the screen.

Inputting information

➲ Click on a cell and type. If the numbers don't fit into the cell hashtags will appear, move the column width to enlarge the space available. If the words don't fit then they will go over the column walls. It is important to enlarge the column to accommodate the words otherwise the column references will become jumbled and not work.

➲ A shortcut to expanding columns or cells is to rest your cursor in between the letters at the top or the numbers at the side and double click. The column or row walls will pop out to accommodate the largest word or number.

➲ To format a set of cells to change the colour or make all numbers appear as money, highlight the set of cells and select the colour (fill bucket) or the money icon (money and coins). This is the way that you can change the cell size, font size or cell borders too.

➲ Inserting images is done the same way as in Word… via the Insert tab.

Calculations

➲ To calculate any set of digits you need to:

   ➲ be able to locate which cell they are in;

   ➲ recognise which operation you need to perform:

   ➲ + = plus, add

   ➲ − = subtract, minus

   ➲ / = divide, share

   ➲ * = multiply

   ➲ Σ = autosum/automatic addition of a set of cells.

➲ Click in an empty cell and **start the formula with an equals sign**

➲ Start the formula with =, click on the cell with the first digit you want to calculate, put in the correct operation and click on the other cell with the digit in.

➲ Press enter on your keyboard and the calculation will be done for you.

➲ Changing the value in the cells will alter the final result.

➲ To copy a formula into the cells below, select the formula cell and then click on the tiny black square in the bottom right hand corner of the cell and drag downwards. The formula will be copied into all the cells below.

➲ Autosum will find a range of cells to add together automatically. You can alter this choice by highlighting your own selection.

Afterword: making it happen – Lorraine Petersen

With the implementation of major SEN and curriculum reforms from September 2014 schools need to address the training requirements of their school workforce. Schools have invested heavily in technology to support their teaching and learning but without high quality professional development all of their investment will be wasted if staff are not using it effectively.

The new SEN Code of Practice is very clear in the message that every teacher is responsible and accountable for every pupil. Although we have many effective, experienced special needs co-ordinators (SENCOs) in our schools, their role is becoming much more strategic and they need to have the knowledge, skills and understanding to support their colleagues. They need the time and resources to manage the SEN provision, to co-ordinate the assessment of pupils and to ensure that the school can meet individual needs.

Teachers often ask how can we motivate learners who have rejected the core curriculum? They ask questions such as, 'I have an autistic child in my classroom and he is completely disengaged. What can I do?' Many of the training programmes see technology as a conduit to the standard curriculum rather than as a subject in its own right. For children with special needs, technology may be the only route into education. It might provide them with access to speech and language, to writing and recording or inspire them with new ways to connect with education. I am always disappointed that so many schools ban phones and PSPs. Yet there is evidence that these are the very tools needed for some children. Decisions made by the leadership team are key to ensuring that the school is meeting the needs of all pupils.

I have gone into primary schools where thousands of pounds of E-Learning credits were spent on software but there is little evidence of the technology being used – when you open the cupboards the boxes fall out. Lack of training meant that the software never got used. There is also the issue of ageing technology. For example, in many authorities the interactive whiteboards and projectors were all installed during the same period and they are all coming to the end of their shelf life at the same time, just when budgets are under pressure. Maintenance may not be a priority so once equipment is old, goes out of fashion or needs repairing, it goes back in the cupboard. Sometimes it just needs a minor adjustment or to be used in a slightly different way and it can be used to benefit groups of children in the school. But how can you improve special needs practice if teachers don't know what's out there or how to use it? How do you provide progression for a child who has grown out of a piece of technology? Parents need to feel confident that all teachers are equipped with the necessary knowledge to support their child and the answer to this lies in effective training.

Whatever resources you put into schools you need to back up with training. Many teachers trained a long time ago when technology was not as advanced or available as it is now. Older teachers may not be ICT savvy and my concern is that as we lose the expertise and support currently offered by local authority personnel, there will be no intermediary to advise and help schools in their purchasing decisions. There is a danger that companies will jump on the bandwagon and sell schools equipment that they don't need and which will not meet the needs of children with special needs.

In the past we have had some very successful training programmes. While some felt there was a postcode lottery and that provision was inconsistent, it did offer some good models for Continuing Professional Development (CPD) for individuals and for whole-school staff development.

Schools also need to be aware that the Equality Duty is explicit in that schools must provide aids and services for those children who need them. How many schools are confident they can meet their legal requirements? Many special schools use technology effectively with pupils who have very profound and complex needs; they need to share their expertise with other schools.

Finally, changes to the ICT curriculum mean a much greater emphasis on computing – are our school workforce trained and equipped for this radical change?

So what can a school do?

⮑ Audit your resources: what have you got and, most importantly, does it work?

⮑ Are all your staff trained in the effective use of technology? What sort of training have they had and how recent?

⮑ What are the needs of the students?

⮑ Match up the teacher skills and pupil needs and decide where the gaps are.

⮑ Develop a strategic plan of what you need to buy in and decide priorities.

⮑ Identify expertise in your local area and find ways of tapping into it. Schools need to work together instead of competing.

Lorraine Petersen OBE (former chief executive of nasen)
Educational Consultant

About the authors

Sal McKeown

These days I earn my living through consultancy and writing, but I taught in schools and colleges for many years and worked with students who had many and varied learning needs from sensory disabilities to mental health issues and autism. My special area of interest is dyslexia although I won the 2006 Journalist of the Year Award for responsible reporting about epilepsy. My 'wow' moment with technology came early on when I worked in adult literacy with people who had severe learning difficulties. Most of this group could only spell a few words and even those were more often wrong than right. We offered work placements to trainee teachers of office skills who ran lunchtime touch-typing classes. Several of the students had a go and I noticed that their spelling improved quite dramatically. They had absorbed patterns through their fingertips and would sit in class, a pen in one hand, while the other hand marked out shapes on the table. ' "Was" is a triangle,' said Sheila, 'and "were" is three steps forward and one back.' This was kinaesthetic learning with a difference and quite a change from drills and skills spelling programmes which were our only strategy at that time. I have been a fan of technology and compensatory strategies ever since. They reach parts of the brain that other teaching will never touch.

➲ For further information see http://www.sallymckeown.co.uk

Angie McGlashon

I have worked in the area of ICT and SEN since joining the special needs support service in Essex in 1983. Before that I had been a primary school teacher for many years, but joining the team enabled me to identify what a fantastic tool we now had to inspire, encourage and enable children with a variety of difficulties to access the curriculum. I always liken it to a jigsaw puzzle; there was the curriculum and there was a struggling pupil and now there was a variety of access and imaginative programmes to enable the child to bridge the gap. I have since worked for a variety of organisations and companies including Widgit software where the power of using images, symbols and visual technologies opened up a whole new means of communication for those who struggled with the conventional text-based approaches. Meeting Sal and sharing her copious knowledge further inspired me to find ways of 'bending' technologies to suit a variety of special needs. I think we are so fortunate to live in a world where people can choose from a range of approaches to participate in the world on an equal level. This book illustrates just how many fantastic ways teachers, carers and people with difficulties can participate in accessing the world around them and enjoy life. I have loved investigating the many new and emerging technologies around at the moment and cannot wait to see what the creative brains of software and hardware companies have to offer us in the future.

➲ For further information see http://edit-training.co.uk/

Index